Understand and Develop Your ESP

BASED ON THE EDGAR CAYCE READINGS

by
Mark A. Thurston

A.R.E. PRESS • VIRGINIA BEACH • VIRGINIA

ACKNOWLEDGEMENTS

The author wishes to acknowledge the invaluable help provided by Charles Thomas Cayce in the preliminary steps of writing this book. That work involved reading together all of the material Edgar Cayce gave on psychic ability and discussing its possible meaning and implications.

In addition, a special thanks is due Doris Dean and Diana Reed for their work in the preparation of the text. Finally, the author wishes to thank Bob Smith for editing the text. The original version of this book (used as an instruction manual for research purposes) was overly technical and more difficult to read. Bob has a special gift for making a complex subject more easily understandable, and his work on this book has been particularly helpful.

CONTENTS

Introduction

The mystery of ESP can be *understood*. We can discover the underlying meaning of experiences like telepathy and clairvoyance. This is a promise found in the Edgar Cayce readings, which contain detailed information to help us with this learning and understanding process.

We can *develop* and *experience* ESP as well. The techniques given in the Edgar Cayce readings are easy to learn, especially when we properly understand how ESP works. However, though these techniques are easy to learn, some people find them difficult to apply. This is because the development of ESP is related to a change in life style and a change in our ways of thinking. But if we will make the effort, the rewards are great. We have an exciting and challenging promise: We can understand and develop our ESP.

Perhaps as much as any other current topic, ESP is leading people to consider the spiritual side of life. Almost everyone has heard of some dramatic instance of mind-to-mind communication or observed an accurate prediction of future events. Even people who admit that they believe in ESP are often startled by these paranormal incidents. Psychic experiences stand out as demonstrations that reality isn't what we often think it is. The very fact that ESP exists is a challenge to us. It forces us to consider the possibility that our minds and our spirits are far greater than we commonly think. However, if properly understood, psychic ability is not for the curiosity seeker; it is for the responsible, sensitive individual who is willing to work at self-discovery.

The reader will notice that the title of this book mentions two aspects of working with psychic ability: understanding and development. It is my hope that in picking up this book you have expressed an interest in both of these topics. However, some of you may be interested only in *understanding* how ESP works. I find that this is true of many students of the Edgar Cayce readings. I, for one, first became interested in the work of the A.R.E. because I wanted to understand how psychic ability operates. What I found in the readings was a very sophisticated and comprehensive theory that explained not only ESP, but also the operation of the mind and the purpose of the soul. I wasn't overly interested in having psychic experiences myself. I was willing to explore things from the intellectual level, yet I felt hesitant to pursue the experiential side of ESP. To a large extent, I was influenced by fellow seekers who warned me that it was easy to get caught up in psychic phenomena and to forget the true purpose of spiritual growth. Even today, I can see that there is a certain degree of truth in that warning. Nevertheless, I have also discovered that there is a place for the development of my psychic ability in the context of spiritual growth and service. And so, I hope that those of you who have picked up this book primarily to understand how ESP works will also read and consider applying the chapters related to the development of psychic ability. In a sense you understand ESP only when you have experienced it from within yourself.

I am also sure that there are readers who are primarily interested in *developing* their psychic gift. I would strongly urge such people to read the first section of this book before moving on to those portions related to the development of ESP. One of the problems with so-called "mind-development courses" is that they do not include a proper foundation or framework within which the individual can develop. However, it is at this point that we find the richness of the Edgar Cayce readings. Not only do they suggest specific procedures and exercises to enhance psychic ability, they also help us to understand what is going on. They allow us to see the way in which ESP can be integrated into daily life and into a broader perspective of unfoldment and growth.

Just as the person who wants to "understand" but not "develop" his or her ESP may be reluctant to experience psychic ability, the person whose primary concern is development often has the characteristic of impatience. We may have read or heard about dramatic demonstrations of psychic ability, and we may deeply desire these in our own lives. Perhaps we have heard stories of individuals who seemingly developed their psychic gift in a matter of days or weeks. However, it is only fair to warn the reader in this introduction that the approaches to psychic development found in the Edgar Cayce readings emphasize the gradual, step-by-step unfoldment of our ESP. The promise is that it can be done, but equally important is the statement that it requires patience.

I would begin by encouraging you to read patiently Part I of this book, which covers the philosophy and theory of psychic ability as it is explained in the Edgar Cayce readings. A rather detailed and complex model of the mechanism of ESP is developed in that section. In connection with this, some parallel reading may be especially helpful to you. One book that I would recommend is *Meditation and the Mind of Man,* which Herbert B. Puryear and I wrote.

Part II of this book, which concerns the development of our ESP, builds upon the concepts and theory presented in Part I. The readings discuss two kinds of activity that can aid in psychic development. The first consists of specific attunement procedures, such as dream study, setting ideals, dietary considerations and meditation, that are meant to be incorporated into a daily life style. For many people, adopting these recommendations will be the most difficult part of developing their psychic gift, because it involves changing old, and sometimes very resistant, habit patterns. You may want to make these changes slowly. Keep in mind that the best psychic development is a gradual, step-by-step process. Some of the specific attunement procedures are described only briefly in this booklet; in such instances you may find it helpful to refer to other A.R.E. publications for greater detail. For example, readers not familiar with the use of castor-oil packs might wish to consult a booklet entitled *Edgar Cayce and the Palma Christi,* by Dr. William A. McGarey, to supplement the material given in these pages.

The second type of development activity discussed in the readings includes exercises which are focused upon enhancing specific aspects of psychic ability. Although it may be tempting to begin with the material in this particular chapter, it will almost undoubtedly prove more productive to work with these developmental exercises in a total context that includes application of the attunement procedures as well.

As a final note, the reader may be interested in knowing how this book was produced. The first draft was prepared for a special research project on psychic ability that was conducted in the fall of 1976 with approximately 400 A.R.E. members taking part. Based upon the comments and suggestions of participants in that study, certain modifications were made in the original manuscript. One significant change was to make the theory and model of ESP derived from the Edgar Cayce readings (described in Chapter Two) less technical and more easily understandable for the general reader. One of the continuing ideals for the research projects that the A.R.E. conducts with its membership is to provide a learning and growth experience for each participant. The first draft of this book was written with the purpose of facilitating such an experience in the lives of those involved in one research study. Those interested in future experiments conducted by the A.R.E. may write the A.R.E. Research Department, Box 595, Virginia Beach, VA 23451.

Glossary

Telepathy—mind-to-mind communication between two individuals under conditions in which it is not possible for information to pass between them through the physical environment using the five senses. Examples: having a hunch that a specific person will unexpectedly call just before he or she does; dreaming about a person and his or her problem although no one has told you about it.

Clairvoyance—conscious awareness of events or conditions that are (1) unknown at that moment to all other minds and (2) removed from the individual to such an extent that no information can be received about them through the environment using the five senses. Examples: a psychic accurately stating where a lost, ancient treasure is buried; Edgar Cayce accurately diagnosing an unknown physical ailment in a person.

Precognition—conscious awareness of an event or condition before it happens (in this case it should be something relatively unpredictable by logic). Examples: guessing correctly many times in a row what number will come up on a randomly tossed die; accurately predicting the exact score of a football game.

Psychokinesis (or PK)—to control or change a condition in the physical world (apart from one's own body) using only the mind. Examples: moving an object on a table using only thought; changing the nature of a solution of chemicals in a flask using only thought directed towards it.

Psi—a shortened form of "psychic ability"; a term used to include any form of ESP (telepathy, clairvoyance and precognition, among others), as well as psychokinesis.

viii

Part I
UNDERSTANDING OUR ESP

The existence of psychic ability has been known to mankind for thousands of years. History tells us that in ancient times, oracles were used in Egypt and in Greece, and the Bible contains numerous accounts of the psychic experiences of such men as Moses and Ezekiel. Historically, the nature of psychic ability has often been closely tied to mankind's understanding of God, for both of these aspects of human experience involve something that comes from beyond our physical sense perceptions. However, psychic ability has not always been equated with messages from divine sources; in fact, in many cases it was considered a primary avenue for demonic forces which were seeking to lead mankind astray. Such beliefs have persisted to the present day in the minds of some. But while it is true that these faculties can be used for selfish or destructive purposes, there seems to be a growing body of information which indicates that psychic ability has tremendous positive applications.

In this century we have seen the tools of modern science applied to the investigation of ESP. This work was begun in earnest in the late 1920s by Dr. J.B. Rhine at Duke University. His work and the research of those who have followed him have demonstrated beyond a reasonable doubt that some people do have verifiable extrasensory perception. This has certainly been an important breakthrough in human understanding, and yet it leaves many unanswered questions which are even more significant:

(1) How does psychic ability work?

(2) What is psychic ability telling us about ourselves?

(3) Is psychic ability in any way related to our search to know God?

Many theories and models have been proposed to try to answer the first question, and some of these will be reviewed later in this section. The work of theorists is very important, because it seems

1

that in our developing understanding of psychic ability, the greatest need at this time is for an exploration of *how ESP works*. Hundreds of research papers attest to the validity of the paranormal, yet more work is needed in constructing a model of how ESP operates if we are to approach an understanding of its implications. Another important need is for greater insight into the relationship between psychic ability and the religious or spiritual experiences that many seekers have reported.

In this book a theory and a model of the mechanism of psychic ability are proposed. This theory of how ESP works is developed from statements in the Edgar Cayce readings, and the model is an attempt to illustrate this mechanism in pictorial form. It is hoped that together they demonstrate a context in which psychic experiences can be understood as a part of evolution in consciousness, or soul growth.

No other psychic has left such an extensive documentation of accurate psychic impressions as has Edgar Cayce. His work, which covered more than 40 years, resulted in over 14,000 transcribed psychic readings. Some of the theories and models of ESP that have previously been proposed by parapsychologists have drawn upon the insights of proven psychics. It is only fitting that the theory contained in the work of America's best-documented psychic also be made known and tested.

There is an additional reason why we need a theory to help us understand ESP. Many people are working with the concepts in the Edgar Cayce readings related to meditation, prayer, dream study and physical attunement. Some find that they have spontaneous psychic experiences. A greater understanding of how and why ESP works would very likely help these people to integrate their experiences into the rest of their spiritual search. Here, taken from hundreds of similar accounts, are four reports of spontaneous experiences of psychic ability that occurred in the lives of individuals working with the attunement procedures recommended in the readings:

> "I have been working with my dreams off and on for six or eight years. I have a friend named B., whom I see once or twice a year. There is only one time that I ever remember dreaming of him. I woke in the middle of the night with a dream that B. was in some kind of restricted situation—a room with others who were upset. I thought in the dream that it might be a mental hospital. I thought

in the dream 'He needs help.' Two weeks later I heard that, in fact, my friend had been admitted to a mental hospital."

"We were sitting in a circle meditating. Directly across from me was a man who I knew had been meditating for many years; he was also a man of strong energies. The energies were moving him from side to side as he sat with his eyes closed. I wondered what was happening in his meditation. By will, I moved into his energy field. It was like stepping into a small twister. All the energies of my body were pushed with great force up into my head. My ears stopped up, my nose stopped up, and my head began to ache. For the next couple of hours I felt as though I had a severe head cold. I learned to stay within my own spiritual space during meditation, and I discovered that even a good vibration from someone else was detrimental when I was opened up to the Christ energy within myself."

"One morning a friend stopped by to see if I needed to fill my water jugs from the well which was about ten miles down the road. I did need to, so after putting my jugs in the car we left. When we got there I picked up a jug in my right hand and my left hand was laid carelessly on top of the open car door. I suddenly gave the door a hard push and the door clicked shut and was closed with my hand caught inside. There I was with a jug in one hand and the other hand caught in the car door. I said to my friend, 'Pauline, open the door, my hand is caught.' She reached over and opened the door. The pain was excruciating and I dreaded to see what I had done. Quick as a flash I ran over to the well and let the water run over my hurt hand. Then I filled my jugs as fast as I could, got back into the car, laid my hand in my lap and looked at it with compassion. Immediately, the broken flesh began to move together, the blood clot was fast disappearing, and at the same time the pain was leaving. Meanwhile, my friend had started the car. I told her to stop the car and look at my hand, which was being healed right in front of my eyes. She stopped the car and watched. She said she had never seen anything like it, and neither had I. In just a few minutes there was no sign of the injury to my hand,

3

not even a scar. It was really wonderful, almost unbelievable unless you saw it as it happened."

"Many inventions or new scientific concepts—such as the sewing machine and the benzene ring in chemistry—are attributed to dreams. It may be that some of these innovations resulted not so much from dreams as from experiences in the hypnogogic state, the state between wakefulness and sleep. The following experience in my own life illustrates such a possibility.

"After years of normal operation my Volkswagen started behaving peculiarly one summer. It would run fine for a block or two, then stop. Only if I let it sit overnight would it restart. I took it to several mechanics and no one could fix the problem. I had given up on it, when one night as I was in the hypnogogic state I had two images come to my mind. In one I was at a self-service gas station removing the gas cap from my car, and as I did there was a 'pop' like the sound of a soft-drink bottle being opened. In the other image I was driving my car and it stopped running—just as it had been doing for some time now.

"I wasn't sure what those images might mean, but when I mentioned them to a friend who is a mechanic he became very excited. He checked the records on my car and discovered that the previous winter the gas tank had been replaced and a newer version had been installed. The tank did not really match the fuel pump in my car. When the weather got hot enough a suction was created in the gas tank (just like the 'pop' I experienced in the hypnogogic image) and my car's fuel pump wasn't able to draw the gas properly. All that was needed was a small hole in the gas cap to keep the suction from occurring. Once we had drilled the hole my car started running fine again."

Chapter One
OTHER THEORIES AND MODELS

One of the most important ways in which we learn is by constructing a theory or a model based upon all known information. These constructions should make certain predictions that are testable through research; based upon the findings of that research, modifications can then be made in the theory or model. This two-stage process has been described by James Connant (1947, p. 37).

In the field of parapsychology more emphasis has been placed upon research than upon theorizing. Most parapsychologists would admit that we have yet to learn and understand fully how ESP works. Nevertheless, there is an extensive body of literature in which various models and theories have been proposed to explain the mechanism of psychic ability. Perhaps the most insightful description of these various theories is found in a book entitled *Experimental Psychology,* by K. Ramakrishna Rao (1966), who has proposed a useful way to categorize the many theories of psi phenomena that have been developed. The six categories recognized in his system are physical, field, collective unconscious, subliminal self, projection, and noncausal theories.

Physical theories suggest that psychic ability can be understood in terms of physical energy transmission. This type of theory, however, faces two major criticisms. First of all, telepathy does not seem to decrease with distance, as we might expect if some particle or wave transmission were involved. And secondly, contrary to what a physical theory would tend to predict, using a Faraday cage to shield the receiver in a telepathy or clairvoyance experiment from electromagnetic waves does not seem to inhibit psychic ability. Despite these problems, some theorists continue to propose physical explanations of ESP. One recent example (Persinger, 1975) suggests that there may be some forms of electromagnetic waves which circumvent the two problems stated above.

A further problem with physical theories concerns the meaning of the word "physical." The history of science demonstrates that the range of things that have been considered physical has steadily expanded. It might be better to use the word "physicalistic" to denote theories that make use of the current understanding of the domain of physical laws. It may well be that certain hypotheses not currently placed in the "physical" category would be so categorized 100 years from now, as our knowledge of the nature of the universe grows.

A second class of theories makes use of the concept of fields. Explanations of this type frequently draw upon sophisticated principles of physics and suggest that every organism has associated with it behavior fields, psi-fields and so forth. Wassermann has proposed a theory (Ciba Foundation Symposium, 1956) which suggests that psi-fields are able to emit and receive very small amounts of energy—so small, in fact, that they are able to be transmitted over long distances without becoming absorbed by matter fields. Another example of a field theory (Murphy, 1945) takes an approach that is in many ways similar to concepts in the readings. It describes psi phenomena (particularly telepathy) as being produced not solely by the individuals who experience them, but rather by the field that exists as all the persons involved act as a whole—through the oneness between them. This theory would predict that states that tend to reduce a sense of personal, ego identity (relaxation states, for example) would enhance the likelihood of having a pyschic experience.

A third group among the theories that have already been proposed involves the collective unconscious. Although Carl Jung preferred to approach psychic phenomena in a noncausal manner through his theory of synchronicity, others have seen in Jung's notion of the collective unconscious a possible mechanism for the transference of psychic impressions. One problem with such theories is that frequently they do not describe the mechanism through which psychic impressions are "selected" from the collective unconscious. Obviously there is an overwhelming amount of information available to each person through the collective unconscious. What distinguishes a good psychic from the average person seems to be the ability to select or choose the accurate psychic material.

A fourth category uses the concept of a subliminal self. This involves an unconscious portion of one's personality capable of receiving extrasensory communication. This subliminal self, with paranormal abilities to receive information, operates beyond the limitations of time and space. According to most such theories, the subliminal self transmits its impressions to conscious awareness through symbolic forms, such as telepathic dreams, mental images and automatic writing.

Closely related to the idea of a subliminal self is the category Rao calls projection theories. Such explanations are based upon the assumption that the *receiver* of extrasensory communication is the active party. According to theories of this type (for example, J.B. Rhine, 1935), at least a portion of the mind is capable of operating independently of the physical body and its time-space limitations. This portion of the mind is able to project itself, to "go out" and take the initiative in obtaining information psychically.

The final category recognized by Rao consists of the noncausal theories. To say that two things are noncausal simply means that one is not causing the other to happen. This tends to be a difficult idea for our logical minds to work with. As mentioned earlier, perhaps the best known of the noncausal theories is Jung's notion of synchronicity. Jung rejected the concept of a causal relationship being operative in psychic experience because he felt that any causal occurrence must involve some form of energy exchange that would be bound by the laws of time and space. There seemed to be clear evidence that some ESP experiences did not operate within these bounds. Synchronicity, or meaningful coincidence, seems most attractive when describing spontaneous psychic events. However, instances involving especially gifted psychics who, like Edgar Cayce, are frequently able at will to complete psychic tasks, would seem to show the limitations of such a theory. Many proposed explanations of precognition would also belong in the noncausal category, since any accurate prediction about the future that is causal in nature would have to be inferential and not precognitive. However, some recent theories (such as Puthoff and Targ, 1974) make use of complex mathematical concepts to explain precognition in a cause-and-effect way.

These six categories do not cover all of the theories that have been proposed. Some especially noteworthy ones have been suggested in the years since Rao's book was written. Rex Stanford (1974) has suggested that the nature of psychic ability may often be to fulfill the needs of the organism and that it often works without one's conscious awareness. Basically, his theory suggests that every person frequently uses psychic ability in an unconscious way to fulfill specific needs. He has also reported research findings that tend to support his theory.

7

Charles Tart (1975) has described a systematic model of the mechanism of ESP, as have Osis and Bokert (1971). A model helps us to organize data and ideas into a convenient and comprehensive format. These models are especially significant in that they clearly identify some of the problems that face parapsychologists in constructing a comprehensive theory of ESP. Among other things, these models describe specific filters within the unconscious mind that can block or distort a psychic impression. We have probably all had some experience with the effects of these filters. From time to time we may have had an intuitive flash, or a hunch, that proved to be partially correct. It is as if the essence of the psychic message was able to get through, but along the way it was distorted or altered in some manner.

Although they cannot be considered theories in the sense that they have led to testable hypotheses, certain teachings from Eastern religions describe psychic ability. For the most part these teachings see psychic powers as a byproduct of the more significant goal of spiritual enlightenment. Lama Govinda (1960) provides an example in his writings on Tibetan Buddhism, in which he states that the awakening of "magical spiritual powers *(siddhi)*" (p. 122) is related to the psychic centers of the body, or *chakras.* However, the body must be understood in terms of five interpenetrating bodies, each consisting of an increasingly more subtle or finer level of energy. This teaching would claim that to undertand how ESP works we need to look beyond just the physical body, which is only the first of these five bodies. Such an idea closely parallels the theory found in the Edgar Cayce readings.

This brief overview of the theories which have already been proposed is not complete. For the reader who wishes to pursue this subject in a more detailed fashion, Rao's book would be an excellent resource. Another helpful book would be *Surveys in Parapsychology,* by Rhea White (1976).

Chapter Two
THE THEORY FROM THE EDGAR CAYCE READINGS
Fundamental Assumptions

Any theory rests upon some basic assumptions. If we wish to construct a theory of how ESP works, we should begin by defining human nature itself. The theory of psychic ability given in the readings of Edgar Cayce is based upon a set of principles which create a foundation for understanding. They provide an explanation of human nature and of the mechanism of ESP and its potential usefulness in our spiritual growth.

Perhaps the most basic of these principles or assumptions is the concept that there exists a universal awareness. This is a state of consciousness that is spiritual in nature—that is, it has the potential to express itself in matter, but it is not limited to time and space. Many terms have been used to describe this universal awareness, such as God, the superconscious and the Creative Forces.

Our relationship to the universal awareness often seems paradoxical. In one way, we are a part of it, for we are part of the whole. And yet, on the other hand, we also experience ourselves as being unique individuals. One aim of spiritual growth is to reconcile this seeming contradiction. Perhaps the best way that we can do this is to begin to express in our individual lives the qualities of the universal. It is a matter of making finite (i.e., making applicable) our infinite nature.

Except for those rare instances of psychic or spiritual experience, our existence as conscious physical beings usually seems to be cut off from the universal awareness. We frequently fail to see the unity of all life, and we tend to see ourselves as independent, although very limited, creatures. The Edgar Cayce readings suggest that when we see ourselves and life in this way, we are failing to take into account unseen, yet very real, aspects of life. One of Edgar Cayce's dreams provided the basis for a model that illustrates this condition.

9

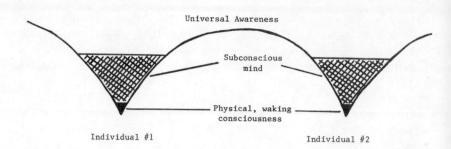

Universal Awareness

Subconscious mind

Physical, waking consciousness

Individual #1   Individual #2

That which cuts us off from the universal awareness is either some element of physical consciousness—such as a conscious attitude or an inharmonious condition in the body—or some aspect of the subconscious mind. By the term "subconscious mind" we are referring to the storehouse of thought patterns which we have created. The word "created" is used here in a very specific way, to indicate that the mind has the capability of giving a shape or a pattern to energy. Although this may sound somewhat strange to us, these thought creations or thought forms are very real and continue to exist even after the thought has left consciousness awareness. The phrase "Thoughts are things," which is found throughout the readings, has special meaning to our understanding of how ESP works.

If we consider our conscious experience in the material world as being three-dimensional, meaning we have a tendency to describe or understand our experiences in the earth in terms of three measurements, we can then assign these thought forms to a fourth-dimensional existence. We find this idea in the Cayce readings as well as in the writings of the Swiss psychiatrist, Carl Jung.

Best definition that ever may be given of fourth dimension is an idea! **364-10**

"If we wish to form a vivid picture of a non-spatial being of the fourth dimension, we should do well to take *thought* as a being for our model."
(Modern Man in Search of a Soul, p. 184)

The reader might wish to refer to Chapter Four of *Meditation and the Mind of Man* for a further explanation of this topic.

The creative capacity of the mind and the existence of its creations at a higher-dimensional level are principles very important to the theory of psychic ability. We should not become confused or intimidated by the introduction of fourth-dimensional reality into the theory, for we all have experiences with our thought-form creations each day. The clearest example of this is dream experiences. We may have a very vivid dream of a place or a group of people that exists not in the physical world, but within our own mental world. At that moment of the dream, however, the experience with these people or that place seems just as real as any waking experience.

The proposition that each individual has within himself universal (or superconscious) awareness depends upon the assumption that each individual is actually a soul. Only a portion of the soul projects itself into the limited dimensions of time and space. The physical body, conscious mind and personality are not apart from the soul, yet they are only a partial representation of it. The remaining aspects of the soul include unconscious elements of the mind, as well as access to universal awareness or the spirit. Perhaps the most important concept in the Edgar Cayce readings concerning psychic ability is that the phenomenon cannot be fully understood if it is approached from only a physical and a mental perspective. The psychic is *of the soul.* Paranormal experiences happen to us because we have a universal, or spiritual, dimension.

The psychic, then, is of the soul, and it operates through faculties of perception, whether hearing, seeing, feeling, or any portions of the sensory system . . . 5752-1

Hence we would have in the truest sense, *psychic,* meaning the expression to the material world of the latent, or hidden sense of the soul and spirit forces, whether manifested from behind, or in and through the material plane. 3744-1

The soul forces within ourselves seek expression, and psychic ability is one form of such expression and should be viewed as a natural experience. It is not a matter of coaxing the soul to manifest itself and its capabilities, for the soul has a constant impulse to express itself in a variety of ways. The problem is to get rid of conditions within the physical consciousness and the subconscious mind that block this natural manifestation.

For, life—or the motivative force of a soul—is eternal; and that portion of same that is motivated by the mental and spiritual attributes of an entity

11

has experienced, does experience the influences that have guided or prompted same through its sojourns.

For each soul seeks expression.   987-4

From the material in the readings we can isolate what seems to be the fundamental requirement for balanced, helpful psychic experiences: attunement. What is needed is an integration of body, mind, and soul. Attunement implies vibration, a term used to describe all of life. The body is a collection of energy made up of various patterns of vibration. Modern physical sciences agree with this point. The readings suggest that the mind and the soul are also expressions of energy that have taken on particular vibrational qualities. In most individuals the vibrational patterns of the body, mind, and soul are not working in an integrated, holistic fashion. Attunement involves the transformation of mental and physical energy conditions, or vibrations, to those of the superconscious awareness of the soul. Whenever attunement is achieved a variety of experiences may arise, including ESP, astral projection and healing.

Q-2. Is there any method whereby I might develop such faculties as a perfect memory; intuition, telepathy, astral projection, and healing of others, as well as myself?

A-2. All healing of every nature comes from the *divine* within that body, or the body applied to such methods or manners of healing.

The attuning of self—not as to that this or that may be accomplished. But remember, as has ever been given of old, *all* manner of expression, all life, emanates from one source—God! God in thyself; not as "I will, but as Thou wilt."

Let that be the purpose, the import, the intent, the *desire;* and that which is needed for the bringing of its abilities and faculties of every nature in attunement will be done.   1861-4

These psychic forces, which are of the soul, are operative not just during paranormal experiences such as ESP or spontaneous healing. The psychic pervades *every* aspect of living, although normally we are not conscious of the way in which we are drawing upon it. Some of the most exciting new findings of parapsychology indicate that we are using our ESP unconsciously in many ways each day. The readings express this principle in the following words.

There is no condition existing in a world as the earth plane but what there is the phenomena in every action of psychic forces manifesting.   900-19

. . . for without the psychic force in the world the physical would be in

that condition of "hit or miss," or that as a ship without a rudder or pilot, for that element that is the guiding force in each and every condition is the spirit or soul of that condition which is the psychic or occult force.

3744-1

If we accept the assumption that we are souls with the potential to bring universal awareness into conscious expression, then psychic ability is seen as a *latent* capability within everyone. In the words of the readings, "These psychic abilities are latent in each and every individual." (256-2) Although the two previously quoted passages from the readings indicate that the psychic is operative in all experience, we should not conclude that everyone has demonstrable ESP that can be called upon at will. This is clearly not the case. Even though psychic perception may be a latent ability in each person, only some people are able consciously to draw upon that potential in a consistent manner. It has been suggested that demonstrable psychic ability may be distributed throughout the population in much the same way as are the other talents, such as musical ability. If this is the case, we will find that some people will score well on ESP tests, about the same number will score correspondingly poorly, and the bulk of the population will show only infrequent or inconsistent psychic ability.

The analogy with musical ability can be used in another way, to illustrate that there are many different types of paranormal capacities, just as there are many different kinds of instruments that can be played. Most likely, there is an underlying similarity in all forms of psychic expressions, just as there are underlying factors upon which is based the talent to play any instrument; however, in our exploration of psychic ability we must not overlook the fact that a particular individual may need to be given a specific kind of ESP task in order to demonstrate his psychic gift.

You find an artiste that is musical; with the ear and sense forces given for the application in the use of some specific instrument. Do you give one that's playing a horn piano lessons? or piano lessons to one that plays the violin?

Not that these are not kindred. Not that these are not in accord. But the expression, the ability to move those forces that manifest themselves, comes through their *particular* phase of expression and manner. 1135-5

It may be tempting to suppose that ESP will result whenever we transcend physical consciousness and that part of the subconscious mind which contains our own thought-form creations. However,

13

this is probably too simple an explanation. The problem arises when we consider more closely the nature of universal awareness. Up to this point in our discussion, universal awareness has been equated with the superconscious mind. The term superconscious (or the mind of the soul) will be used in the rest of this book to denote the *highest* state of awareness, which is totally unlimited. In addition to the superconscious, there are other levels of awareness that might be termed "universal" in the sense that they transcend time and space, and in the sense that they are universally accessible, available to all individuals. However, in contrast to superconscious awareness, which is defined as being unlimited and omniscient, each of these levels of awareness has distinct limitations. Some of these lesser levels of universal awareness are the collective unconscious, the astral plane, and the etheric plane, to name just a few. To depict this condition, we might redraw our original model as follows:

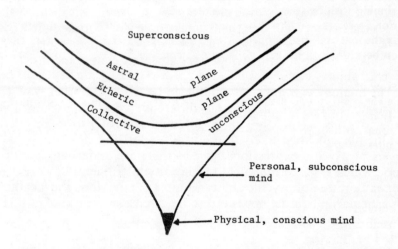

Psychic impressions can come from any of these levels. For example, we can have psychic experiences involving the astral level, like those in which we attune ourselves to another person's thought-form creations, which are at that level. Such experiences may include attuning oneself to discarnate souls, as demonstrated in mediumship. The Edgar Cayce readings emphasize the importance of attuning oneself to the consciousness of superconscious awareness, for it is at this level that the limitations and inaccuracies of the lower levels are transcended.

14

A considerable amount of material concerning the actual development of psychic ability will be presented in this booklet. However, in this section on fundamental assumptions it will be helpful to consider two basic positions taken by the readings regarding psychic capacities. The first is that paranormal abilities are awakened as a *natural result* of the proper motivation: to grow in spiritual awareness and in service to others. This is in distinction to the common desire to develop psychic ability in order to be able to impress others or oneself with remarkable phenomena (for example, mind reading just for the sake of curiosity and without an altruistic purpose). We find the principle that ESP will be a natural outgrowth in the following passages from the readings:

Q-6. How may I develop psychic power for warnings of danger, difficulties to be avoided and opportunities to be taken advantage of, for myself, my children and others?
A-6. Let these be rather the outgrowth of the spiritual desire, rather than beginning with material manifestations, see?

For, these *are*—to be sure—a part of the whole, but if they are sought for only the material sustenance, material warning, material satisfaction, they soon become dead in their ability to be creative.   1947-3

How develop the psychic forces? So live in body, in mind, that self may be a channel through which the Creative Forces *may* run . . . So with the body mentally, physically, spiritually, so make the body, the mind, the spiritual influences, a channel—and the *natural* consequences will be the manifestations.   5752-2

The second basic position concerns the question of why some people have ESP and some do not. In the readings we find the theory of reincarnation as a part of the description of how souls evolve in consciousness. This theory helps us answer an obvious question raised by the first basic position on psychic development: How are we to account for people who have clearly demonstrable psychic ability and yet have no desire to use it for the benefit of others or for their own spiritual growth? The readings suggest that many individuals have developed psychic capacities in previous earthly experiences, especially during those time periods in which paranormal abilities were respected in the culture and used to benefit society. Although these experiences may not be consciously remembered, the qualities developed can be drawn upon, just as a child prodigy in music or mathematics, like Mozart or Pascal, is able to draw upon his or her previous development.

A term used in the readings to refer to abilities that were developed in previous lives is "innate." This term should not be confused with "latent," which indicates the potential in everyone yet does not signify that the ability has been previously brought into conscious use.

There are those in the group who have experimented that are gifted; gifted meaning then *innately* developed by the use of those faculties of the Mind to attune themselves to the Infinite.   792-2

The theory of reincarnation has another significant role in our examination of the fundamental assumptions about psychic ability, in that it can provide us with a more enlightened historical perspective. The readings suggest that an ancient civilization called Atlantis was destroyed more than 12,000 years ago—destruction due at least partially to the misuse of psychic abilities. Many individuals who received readings from Edgar Cayce were told that they had had incarnations in this society at the time of the destructions. This information seems pertinent to our consideration of psychic ability, because the readings indicate that mankind once again stands at a crossroads. Once more we have the technology with which to destroy ourselves. We are also discovering the tremendous psychic powers of the mind, which can be used constructively or destructively. Every helpful influence possible must be brought to bear on conditions in our world if we are to avert another destruction of a major portion of mankind. The importance of modern man gaining a thorough understanding of the mechanism and purpose of psychic ability cannot be underestimated. The spiritual implications of psychic ability may well provide one of the most stabilizing and healing forces possible.

The Mechanism of Psychic Ability

In this section we will turn our attention to a theory of how psychic ability operates. Here we will be interested in defining the primary factors that are involved and the ways in which these factors can relate to each other. When we finish, we will have a rather complex model which (a) takes into account the theory given in the Edgar Cayce readings, (b) accounts for many previous parapsychological findings, and (c) predicts the nature of certain parapsychological relationships that have not yet been researched.

Any model is, of course, only an approximation of reality. It is very likely that every factor within our model of psychic ability has some kind of influence on every other factor. However, for our present purposes, we will be concerned with only those relationships which seem to have a significant, direct bearing on psychic experiences.

Physical consciousness

Our normal waking physical consciousness is produced primarily by our bodies and especially by the sensory input that they receive from the physical environment. Research studies have shown that under conditions of sensory deprivation, in which the body's senses are able to receive virtually no stimulation, normal physical consciousness is interrupted and an altered state of consciousness is produced. We might conclude, therefore, that an important factor in maintaining normal waking consciousness is the reception of outside stimuli by the senses of the body. Of course, this waking state of consciousness is necessary because it allows us to make our behavior appropriate to daily life in the physical world.

However, we must remember that the five senses do not actually function at the conscious level. They operate in a relatively unconscious and automatic way, and we become aware of only a small portion of what they receive. For example, as you were reading the previous paragraph, your senses undoubtedly received sounds, smells and sights that did not pass into your conscious awareness. If we were to draw a model of our normal waking consciousness, it would look something like this:

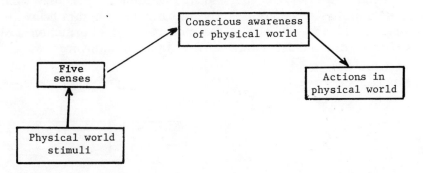

According to the readings, the senses have another important role in addition to helping us to become aware of what is happening in the outer world: They also help us to become conscious of inner events, including psychic impressions.

17

The psychic, then, is of the soul, and it operates through faculties of perception, whether hearing, seeing, feeling, or any portions of the sensory system . . .   5752-1

Awareness of subjective, inner events

Of course, our awareness is not always focused upon the outside world; we can also become aware of impressions that come from within. The variety of these inner impressions is extensive, ranging from memories of recent events to accurate psychic impressions. The readings tell us that the senses, together with special parts of the nervous system located mainly in the brain, form a receiver that can pick up both environmental stimuli and inner impressions. What frequently happens, however, is that information from the physical environment overrides or cuts off our awareness of impressions from within. For example, imagine that you are driving through heavy traffic in an unfamiliar part of town. It is unlikely that in such a situation you would be consciously attending to random memories or other subjective, inner impressions. You would be primarily concerned with evaluating information coming to you from the environment. One exception to this would be a memory that is directly helpful to you in dealing with your current situation, like, for instance, remembering that a particular traffic sign has a special meaning. What determines or selects the information that is allowed to pass into our conscious awareness? As we have noted, this receiver is constantly being bombarded with environmental stimuli as well as inner impressions. Among the major factors in this selection process are our ideals, attitudes, purposes and motivations. The situation is illustrated in the diagram below, in which solid arrows indicate the movement of information and dotted arrows indicate controlling or directing influences.

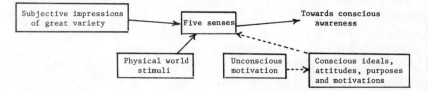

A considerable amount of research has been done on the question of how awareness is related to attitudes and motivation. However, when we examine motivations it is often difficult to determine which are conscious and which are unconscious. It may well be that most experiences of the conscious mind are in fact built upon influences

18

that remain unconscious. An example of this can be seen in the case of a person who tries overly hard to do well at his job, but whose drive comes from an unconscious motivation to make up for feelings of inadequacy from childhood.

We have probably all had some experience with the way in which an attitude or a motivation can clearly affect our conscious awareness. For example, suppose you are taking an important test and you need to remember some obscure name or date. If you are motivated to do well on the test, you will probably minimize for a few moments the attention you give your physical environment, while you allow subjective memories to occupy your awareness. However, the Edgar Cayce readings go further and suggest that if you hold in mind particular attitudes and purposes, you may make it more likely that you will become aware of another category of subjective impressions: accurate psychic information. In the above example, this information might come as thought transference from a person who knows the correct answer or from superconscious awareness, where all knowledge is available.

The question, of course, arises as to the nature of those particular attitudes and purposes that will facilitate psychic ability. The most carefully researched answer to this question is "the belief that ESP is possible." It has been clearly demonstrated in many studies that subjects who believe in ESP are more likely to do well on ESP tasks. It could be argued that some of this effect is due to the fact that many people who believe in ESP do so because they have had frequent personal experiences with it, and hence they would be more likely to perform psychic tasks well; however, it is unlikely that this accounts for all of the effect. It is also important to remember that simply our openness to the possibility of an experience can make it more likely that the experience will be recognized when it stands at the threshold of our conscious awareness. For example, suppose you had a dream in which you saw an old friend in a crowd of people. If you intuitively felt that this was actually a precognitive—or prophetic— dream, and that this old friend might very well be in your town soon, then you might keep an eye out for him. Walking through a crowded store several days later you might actually pass near him, and you would be more likely to notice him because you were open for the experience. Your conscious attitude and motivation would make you especially alert to a particular kind of impression. In this case the impression was visual (the face of your friend), but the same principle holds true for more subjective impressions, such as psychic ones.

The Edgar Cayce readings suggest another conscious attitude or purpose which will facilitate psychic ability: a desire to help others. This principle has already been discussed. We cannot claim that this desire is a sufficient condition in itself for the awakening of psychic ability. Nevertheless, it may influence the selection process that takes place as a wide variety of impressions impinge upon the sensory system. The desire to help will probably make it more likely that information coming from universal awareness or from another person's mind will be allowed to pass into conscious awareness. In the following passage one individual is counseled that unless he is grounded in universal motivation, unless his goal is to serve and to experience the unity of all life, the subjective impressions he expects to be accurate psychic information actually are more likely to be elements of his own imagination.

In giving the interpretation of that which *is* received through these higher activities of the sensory forces of a body is oft where individuals may bring their *own* imaginative forces, or the satisfying of their individual ego to be above that of or exceptional to others, to such a point that there may be the satisfying of that within the self.

Why, then, is this all to be taken into consideration from that as has been given in aiding or instructing individuals in development of these faculties?

For there remains, ever, the universal law that comes as the basis of man's relationships to the Creative Forces; that first law, that thou shalt not have any god before thee other than that thou wilt worship in Him!

Hence unless such an individual, that shows a tendency, is grounded in that which *is* the universal motivative force that *can* be *constructive,* it becomes rather among those that allow the influences to enter that are not only the exaltation of personal ego but the exaltation of personal egos that may be in a state of *positive* affluence through the very opening of self for such a manifestation.   1135-3

A second important reason for holding a conscious attitude of service is that without such a selfless motive the awakening of psychic ability is more likely to be a confusing or disorienting experience. So many of our life experiences that seem confusing have this quality because they do not have a purposefulness which seems meaningful. For example, an individual who gets intoxicated every Saturday night may begin to find that this experience is no longer fun and has become confusing and disorienting. One possible reason for his feeling of confusion is related to a lack of purpose behind this particular activity. In the following reading we find the advice that we should have a purpose beyond ourselves as we work with psychic ability (which is referred to here as expressing our "super-selves").

Know that the seeking, the developing of individuals in the expression of their super-selves in their activity must be for *creative* forces and not (as *this* entity now called [1135] has seen, has *known* in its *inner* self) for self-aggrandizement, self-exaltation, self-indulgence; for if it is, then the *way* of that soul is made all the more in a state of bewilderment—without a cause.
1135-2

The previous diagram from our model illustrates how important the sensory system is to understanding how psychic ability works. One key to the development of psychic ability seems to be to interrupt the way that impressions are usually sorted at this point. We have just examined one way of effecting this kind of alteration: through our conscious attitudes and motivations. Another method—perhaps more straightforward—is to change the amount of sensory stimuli coming from the physical environment. This is called sensory deprivation, and it was mentioned briefly in the section on physical consciousness. Sensory deprivation usually does not refer to blocking stimuli from just one of the senses. For example, someone who is blind has the input channel of sight cut off but usually makes an adjustment by becoming more sensitive to one of the other channels, such as the sense of hearing. Sensory-deprivation experiments usually involves cutting off as many of the senses as possible; this can be done by floating a person in body-temperature salt water in a sound- and lightproof room. John Lilly (1972) and others have reported paranormal experiences under such conditions.

An alternative method to blocking out all environmental stimuli is to alter the nature of the stimuli. There is some evidence to indicate that a repetitious input from the environment serves to interrupt the way in which the senses operate, and this may allow psychic impressions to come into awareness. Charles Honorton and Sharon Harper (1974) have reported significant telepathy scores for subjects who received a constant visual and auditory stimulus. Meditators who chant their mantra for a long period of time, thus providing themselves with a repetitive auditory stimulus, report attaining an altered state of consciousness, although it is not clear that this results in verifiable ESP. The Edgar Cayce readings support the principle that paranormal experiences can result from (a) altering the input of environmental impressions and (b) using the senses as a vehicle of expression for inner events.

21

In the material manifestations, concepts are made aware to observers—and the more oft to the individual—through a functioning of the senses; or the perception is arrived at through such activity.

Hence there are those varied forms of demonstrative activity; as in the vision without the sense of the natural eye; the perception of hearing without the activity of the auditory forces of the natural body. There is also the feeling without those perceptions of the personal or physical contact by a presence. There is a super-activity through the olfactory centers that produces perception.   1135-3

Each will find a variation according to the application and the abilities of each to become less and less controlled by personality, and the more and more able to shut away the material consciousness—or the mind portion that is of the material, propagated or implied by what is termed the five senses. The more and more each is impelled by that which is intuitive, or the relying upon the soul force within, the greater, the farther, the deeper, the broader, the more constructive may be the result.   792-2

To summarize this section, we have explored the concept that at least two important mechanisms must be operative in conjunction with the senses if we are to experience conscious psychic ability. First, we must allow subjective impressions to enter our awareness. This can be facilitated by sensory deprivation or by making the relationship between the senses and the physical environment repetitive or automatic. Secondly, we must select from the wide variety of subjective impressions that are available those that are actually coming from beyond our own imaginings or memories. Among the factors important in this selection process are our conscious and unconscious attitudes, purposes and motivations. Other factors no doubt are involved as well. One that we will explore later is the condition of the physical body.

A higher-dimensional receiver

This section will describe one of the readings' most significant concepts concerning how our ESP works, a concept that relates to the nature of the physical body. According to the Cayce material, at least two aspects of the physical body are involved in ESP. First there is the "flesh body," which, because it is easily measured and its presence easily detected, is very familiar to us; we can see our own bodies or the bodies of others, and, even if we are blind, we can become aware of the flesh body through one of the other senses. Secondly, the readings indicate that each flesh body is accompanied by another aspect of the physical body, referred to as the "finer

22

physical body." Like the flesh body, the finer physical body is an energy system. The two energy systems are closely related, and together they work in an integrated manner to make up the physical person. The fact that most people cannot see this finer physical body should not lead us to the conclusion that it does not exist.

Traditional science has provided us with some evidence of the finer physical body. Medical doctors are frequently baffled by cases of so-called "spontaneous remission," in which there seems to be no justification within the flesh body for a healing to have taken place. It may well be that such cases involve the direct activity of the finer physical body. As further evidence of the existence of this structure, several psychics have been well documented in laboratory settings in their ability to diagnose patients accurately, simply by observing this finer physical body. They describe seeing energy patterns surrounding and interpenetrating the flesh body, a phenomenon that is often referred to as the "aura" (see Karagulla, 1967). Another significant area of research involves out-of-body experiences. These studies seem to indicate that each individual has a higher-vibrational body, which is normally invisible to human vision and can separate from the flesh body and undergo experiences in a relatively independent manner. Although there is not yet enough evidence to convince everyone of the reality of these out-of-body experiences, a growing collection of research findings supports this notion. It may have far-reaching implications for medicine as well as for our understanding of how psychic ability works.

The finer physical body plays an extremely important role in our theory of psychic ability. The readings suggest that it is capable of receiving impressions that are not of the material world. The reader will recall that some theorists have proposed a physical explanation for ESP. If these theories are accurate, we would need to find some aspect of the flesh body capable of receiving a wave or particle carrying ESP information. Up until now, the search for such a receiver has been fruitless. The Edgar Cayce readings suggest that the transference of psychic impressions does not take place at the level of the material world and that something other than the flesh body receives such impressions.

The finer physical body can be thought of as that receiver. It is sensitive to energy patterns of a higher-dimensional level: fourth-dimensional, thought-form creations. Although such a concept may seem rather abstract to many readers, it helps to explain much of the mystery of psychic ability. The finer physical body extends beyond the limitations of time and space, as do certain psychic phenomena.

Most simply stated, the theory given in the Edgar Cayce readings suggests that a finer physical body (closely related to the flesh body) can receive or is sensitive to thought, either one's own thoughts or those of others. Of course, this would explain only telepathy, and we will see that another source of information is also accessible to the finer physical body.

At this point an illustration might be helpful. Since some of the qualities of the finer physical body are fourth-dimensional, it is extremely difficult to depict them in a two-dimensional diagram. To help us understand the finer physical body, we might use an analogy. In this analogy we can suppose that the three-dimensional world of time and space, in which we normally operate, is like a two-dimensional piece of paper. Contained within that world of time and space is the flesh body. The finer physical body, which is depicted on the right-hand side of the diagram below, is of one greater dimension than the flesh body. Notice that in a sense the finer physical body interpenetrates the flesh body; it is as if one cross section of the finer physical body roughly corresponds to the flesh body. This diagram clearly illustrates an important point: Whereas the flesh body is relatively limited in sensitivity and would usually receive impressions from only the material level of time and space, the finer physical body has far greater sensitivity. We might imagine, in our diagram, other two-dimensional pieces of paper intersecting the finer physical body. These would represent other planes or dimensions of consciousness from which the finer physical body could receive psychic impressions.

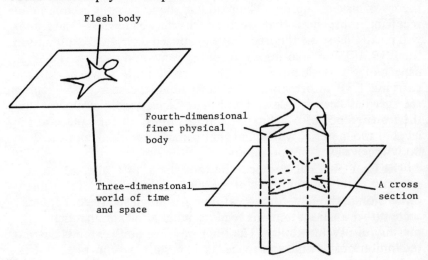

Flesh body

Fourth-dimensional finer physical body

Three-dimensional world of time and space

A cross section

Of further interest is the relationship of the finer physical body to health. The cross section of the finer physical body that exists in the material realm very closely approximates the conditions of the flesh body. It is often a precursor of conditions experienced in the flesh; in other words, a disturbance within the finer physical body would probably lead to a disturbance in the flesh body at a later time, seconds or even months later. Another characteristic of the finer physical body is that it is always fully intact, whereas the flesh body may not be. For example, even though an individual may have had an arm amputated, the corresponding arm in the finer physical body would still be there. The readings suggest, as well, that prayer for healing affects another person first through the finer physical body, with the effect then moving to the flesh body.

If, in fact, the finer physical body is capable of receiving information not accessible to the flesh body, we should consider the possible sources of that information. The readings describe three sources from which such information can be received. First is universal awareness, or, more specifically, that portion of it that we have labeled the superconscious mind. The second possible source is an individual's own thought forms—for example, impressions that we receive from our own imaginations. The third source is the thought forms of another person. However, as illustrated in the diagram below, this information must first pass through the personal thought forms of the receiver. Such a transmission may take place at lower levels of universal awareness, such as the collective unconscious or the astral plane.

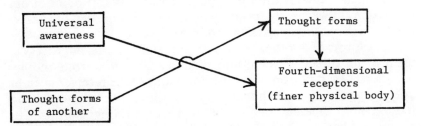

As we might expect, the readings state that the most accurate and helpful form of psychic ability involves the finer physical body receiving information from the superconscious. This is because at the superconscious level we are free of the limitations and distortions that characterize the lower levels of the mind. By attuning ourselves to the superconscious we may in fact receive divine guidance and direction from the soul.

When the information being received by the finer physical body comes only from an individual's *own* thought forms, the result is not psychic ability but the possibility for conscious awareness of memories or imaginings. We find this condition described in a passage we considered earlier.

In giving the interpretation of that which *is* received through these higher activities of the sensory forces of a body is oft where individuals may bring their *own* imaginative forces, or the satisfying of their individual ego to be above that of or exceptional to others, to such a point that there may be the satisfying of that within the self. 1135-3

This also seems to be the condition described in the following statement to an individual who sought advice about being more psychic. In this case, the reference to "mental-material visioning" can be interpreted to mean that this individual was not allowing himself to become receptive to outside information. Instead, he was making guesses based primarily on his own efforts to use the physical conscious mind to imagine the target.

There is the tendency for world wisdom to confound the spiritual concept. Hence most of the common experiences become guesses, or the attempt to vision by mental-material visioning. 792-2

In a later section, as part of an investigation of the role of the sender in telepathic communication, we will consider the factors that influence the creation of thought forms. At this point in our discussion, however, the primary concern is the variety of sources from which the finer physical body can receive information. The thought forms of another person are one such source, but access to them is not direct. Psychic information that comes from another person rather than from the superconscious of the receiver must be interpreted through the thought forms of the receiver; therefore, in a sense it must "match" one of his or her own thought forms. The precise mechanism of this "matching" is not clearly spelled out in the Edgar Cayce readings. However, we are given the basic principle that the information being directly received from another person must be translated into terms that the receiver can consciously understand. If we imagine that there is a language of the unconscious, then each person speaks a different dialect of that language. To the extent that the message being transmitted involves words that are pronounced in a similar way in the dialects of the sender and the receiver, the message is more likely to be accurately received. Here is one reason why we might expect greater ESP between family members. Not only is it probable that they will be motivated by love, but they are also likely to have had similar experiences and thus, to a large degree, to have similar thought forms available.

Attunement of the finer physical body

We have seen that there are three primary sources of information from which the receivers within the finer physical body can draw. There are, in addition, at least two important factors that determine which of these sources is drawn upon. The first is the individual's conscious attitudes and purposes; the second is the attunement level of the spiritual centers. We have already explored the first factor and found that the readings suggest that self-centered attitudes and purposes tend to orient these receivers towards one's *own* thought forms. On the other hand, a conscious ideal and purpose of service and caring for others makes a person more likely to be able to psychically draw upon information from the superconscious or from another person.

The spiritual centers (or *chakras,* to use Eastern terminology) are located within the finer physical body. These centers are the seven locations within the body that especially control the integration and alignment of the physical, mental and spiritual aspects of our being. Many books based upon the Edgar Cayce readings and many other sources have been written concerning the spiritual centers. Anyone who wishes to explore this area in greater depth will find many resources available, including *Meditation— Gateway to Light* and *Meditation and the Mind of Man,* both available from the A.R.E. Press. However, for purposes of understanding how ESP works, the following three points are most significant:

1. The spiritual centers act as a bridge between our conscious, physical selves and the psychic or spiritual parts of our being. They act as a mediator between our finite lives in materiality and our infinite lives as souls.

2. Each of the seven spiritual centers relates to a different aspect of consciousness and experience. In terms of our understanding of ESP, a particular type of psychic experience is related to each of the spiritual centers. Of course, in any type of experience, psychic or otherwise, there is likely to be a combination of the activities of

27

several centers. However, specific forms of psychic ability have often been associated especially with a particular center. For example, as the third spiritual center, located in the area of the solar plexus and adrenal glands, is awakened or "opened," we are likely to observe mediumship abilities. Similarly, poltergeist phenomena may be related to the cells of Leydig and/or gonad centers, and glossolalia (speaking in tongues) seems to be related to the thyroid center. *Ideally,* these seven spiritual centers will operate in an integrated, cooperative fashion. When this happens, the resulting psychic ability is more likely to come from superconscious awareness.

3. Thought creations of our minds have a special relationship to the individual spiritual centers. Some people have even used the expression that our thought forms are "stored within the centers." We have probably all observed that through our conscious attitudes and our behavior in daily life, we tend to activate or awaken particular memories. These memories can be thought of as examples of our thought forms, and the readings suggest that specific types of thought-form memories tend to be associated with particular spiritual centers.

This concept may have a direct bearing on our ability to receive information psychically. For example, the second spiritual center relates to our consciousness and experience of the male-female balance, including our attitudes and physical expression in sexual activity. Male college students often spend a considerable amount of time focusing on this subject, so from our theory we would predict that their own thought forms about sexuality would be particularly accessible and easily able to come into their conscious awareness. The reader will recall that one phase of the finer physical body's reception of telepathic impressions involves having the thought form of the sender "match" accessible thought forms of the receiver. Considering this statement in combination with the preceding one, we might expect male college students to do better on ESP tests when the target pictures are erotic in nature rather than of a more commonplace type; research findings have indicated that this is, in fact, frequently the case. We might suspect that this principle could be shown to hold true for female college students as well.

The concept that memory patterns may be especially important to the mechanism of telepathy has been pointed out by parapsychologists. Honorton and Harper (1974) found that telepathic impressions were often received in images that matched available memories. They write, "Memory, in particular, seems to serve as a vehicle for psi-mediation" (1974, p. 164).

This discussion of the spiritual centers may help us to understand why the readings suggest that meditation would help an individual to develop psychic ability. In the first place, meditation tends to awaken the activities of the spiritual centers, particularly those of the three highest ones. These three highest centers are directly related to our awareness of ourselves as souls. Since all of the centers are mediators between our physical, conscious selves and the more unlimited levels of the soul, the awakening of their activity in meditation may result in psychic experiences. This is especially true if we meditate upon a spiritual ideal, which would help to integrate the activities of all seven centers.

Second, psychic ability may be developed as our attitudes and purposes are transformed through proper meditation. We may move from self-centeredness to love, which will help us to attune to information which comes from beyond our own imaginings and desires.

And third, meditation may help to awaken constructive, helpful experiences of psychic ability as we realign and integrate the activities of the spiritual centers and their corresponding thought forms. Many schools of meditation teach that such a reprogramming of the activities of these centers is an important byproduct of meditation. When such attunement and integration has taken place in all of our centers, we might expect to be sensitive to a wider range of psychic impressions than were the male college students mentioned in the previous example.

A summary of factors affecting the attunement of the finer physical body is shown in the following diagram. Once again, the dotted lines indicate controlling or directing influences. The solid-lined arrow between "thought forms" and "spiritual centers" represents the concept that particular thought forms are directly associated with specific spiritual centers.

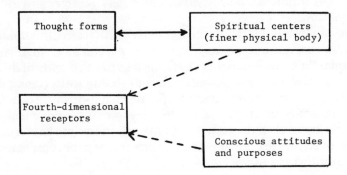

Filtering factors

This portion of our model relates to unconscious factors within the mind that lie between the receivers of the finer physical body and the sensory system of the flesh body and conscious mind. The unconscious mind has access to information received by the finer physical body, just as the conscious mind can get information through the flesh body's senses. However, certain stages must be passed through for this unconscious material to reach conscious awareness. These stages, or filtering mechanisms, are often advantageous because we probably would not want to become aware of every psychic impression available to us. Our awareness would be swamped, just as it would be if we became aware of every possible sensory stimulus that reached the flesh body.

What are the stages involved in a psychic impression moving from the receiver of the finer physical body to conscious awareness? Karlis Osis and Edwin Bokert (1971) have proposed an excellent model for understanding this internal processing. There is nothing in the Edgar Cayce readings to suggest any modifications of their proposal, and it is incorporated into our overall model as is.

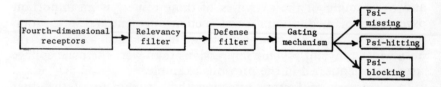

The relevancy filter "protects the organism from information overload" by screening out irrelevant or unnecessary information. For example, at this moment you may potentially have access to telepathic information concerning the activities of a neighbor. However, if those activities don't really have a bearing on your own life at this moment, the relevancy filter may be screening out that information.

The defense filter protects an individual from threatening or painful information he might receive psychically, such as, for example, the knowledge that someone else has thoughts of disliking him. The relevancy and defense filters probably work together. For instance, if something catastrophic were happening to a family member hundreds of miles away, the awareness of that event might be quite painful; but the tremendous relevancy of the occurrence could override the unconscious reluctance to become aware of painful information.

It is likely that another mechanism blocks many ESP impressions, not because they contain distressing news about others, but because they threaten the world view that is usually held. For example, if I were to become aware that I can tune in on other people's thoughts, I could not ignore the implication that they can potentially tune in on mine, as well. Since I may not want to have to face the fact that my secret thoughts can be known, it may be safer to block my own ESP impressions and preserve the traditional world view that ESP is impossible. We can call this aspect of the process "psi-blocking."

The same mechanism that causes psi-blocking—which we can label the "gating mechanism"—could also prevent accurate psychic impressions from coming to conscious awareness by distorting the impressions. The most straightforward way this could take place in the unconscious mind would be for one's ESP to be used to miss the correct target in a consistent way—that is, "psi-missing." This is *not* to say that every time a person tries to demonstrate ESP and is wrong it is psi-missing. We use this term only to describe a situation in which a person is wrong so frequently that it is statistically very unlikely to be due to chance. For example, if a person is asked to telepathically guess a standard deck of ESP symbols card by card, and he misses *every one,* this is a meaningful demonstration of psychic ability. It is very unlikely that chance alone would cause him to miss continually. It has been found that when a subject has an unsympathetic attitude towards ESP in general or towards the specific ESP task at hand, psi-missing is likely to occur.

In addition to psi-blocking and psi-missing, a third possibility exists at the gating mechanism: psi-hitting, or allowing the impression to come through undistorted. It is this possibility that we will continue to focus our attention upon as we develop our model of how psychic ability works.

Attunement of the flesh body

As we have already seen in developing the theory of psychic ability found in the readings, the sensory system of the physical body has an especially important role to play. A previous description was given of two basic types of information which can be received by the sensory system: stimuli from the physical world and mental impressions (some of which might be psychic) from inner, subjective levels. It was also pointed out that a person's conscious ideals, purposes and motivations have a controlling influence on the type of impressions that are selected to come into conscious awareness.

31

Another extremely important controlling factor is the general health and balance of the physical body. This concept is depicted in the following diagram:

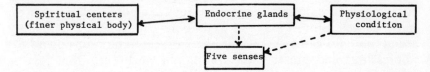

Seven of the endocrine glands—the gonads, cells of Leydig, adrenals, thymus, thyroid, pineal and pituitary glands—have a special relationship to the spiritual centers of the finer physical body: Each of these glands serves as a part of one of the centers. For example, the pineal is the expression in the flesh body of the sixth spiritual center. The nonflesh components of the center are found within the finer physical body. This concept is *symbolically* illustrated in the following diagram:

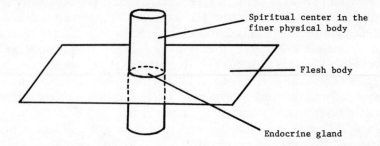

As we can see from the above diagram, anything which affects the endocrine gland is likely to influence the total functioning of that particular spiritual center, and vice-versa. Furthermore, as the research findings of endocrinology have shown, the general condition of the physical body, especially of the nervous system, has an extensive effect on the operation of the endocrine centers and the sensory system.

In order to understand how the flesh body can be attuned and how that attunement might affect psychic ability, it is necessary to consider first three different ways in which psychic ability can arise. The following distinctions are undoubtedly one of the most significant aspects of the theory of psychic ability found in the readings. The Cayce material is one of the few sources to differentiate clearly between a variety of conditions that can produce a psychic gift.

1. Making use of the theory of reincarnation, the readings suggest that psychic ability may be related to experiences in previous lifetimes. By working with such attunement procedures as meditation, an individual may have developed a psychic gift during a former incarnation. That soul would still have memory patterns related to this ability and would perhaps be capable of drawing upon those patterns during the current lifetime, even though a conscious attitude of service or spiritual seeking may no longer be held; thus we would have a type of residual effect. Apparently the spiritual centers and the associated thought forms retain, at least temporarily, the memory of functioning in such a way as to allow accurate psychic impressions to come through.

2. An imbalanced condition in the flesh body can also cause psychic ability. This is especially true of situations in which stress is placed on one of the endocrine glands. This stress results in the activation of the corresponding spiritual center of the finer physical body, thus potentially opening a channel in that individual for psychic experiences to occur. Unfortunately, these experiences may be imbalanced or confused, as are the physiological conditions that create them. This theory gives us a way of interpreting the psychic experiences that may occur under the influence of hallucinogenic drugs. Through the activity of these drugs on the chemistry of the brain and related endocrine glands, a temporary stressful or hyperstimulated condition, which can have a direct effect on the spiritual centers, may come about.

This theory is further illustrated in the case histories of individuals who have developed psychic ability immediately after incurring an injury to the nervous system. The classic example of this is Peter Hurkos, who became aware of his psychic gift after an accident in which he fell on his head. Our theory would suggest that the injury created an imbalanced or stressful condition in one of the endocrine glands, most likely the pineal or pituitary.

3. A balanced and attuned condition among the various aspects of the flesh body can also have a direct, positive effect on the development of psychic ability. This effect can be twofold. First, an attuned, balanced body will make for a more sensitive, alert condition in the five senses. In addition, the integrated, harmonious operation of the endocrine glands allows the spiritual centers to function in a corresponding way. When this is the case, the psychic experiences that may result are more likely to be balanced and helpful. They come not from the awakening of just one center, but from a holistic, healthy state of being. Specific recommendations

from the readings for the attunement of the flesh body are found in Chapter Three of this book. They include dietary procedures, exercise and other activities designed to create a greater physical balance.

It is unfortunate that the differences among these three origins of psychic ability are not clear in most people's minds. Our concern has been to categorize an experience in terms of telepathy, clairvoyance or precognition, instead of in terms of the conditions that produced it. This has caused confusion in parapsychology, because we often find three different kinds of individuals who seem to be having experiences that are similar in many ways. The following excerpt from the readings uses an analogy to distinguish between psychic experiences that arise from imbalanced conditions and those that come from attunement: One is like an appliance that has shorted out and may be demonstrating unusual behavior, while the other is like a radio that has been carefully tuned to the desired frequency.

In electrical forces of every nature (that are the very basis of the atomic structure of the body, through which there is the manifestation of mind and soul of an individual entity, in its varied forms of *whatever* nature), if there are shorts of any nature there is confusion. This is true whether it be in the atomic structure of the individual or in any mechanical appliance to which it may be applied for its activity in the relationships for the benefit or convenience or constructive forces for man.

So in the radio wave that may make for pleasure, for convenience, for activities that are necessary for an attunement to a vibratory rate of a given nature for its association or connection with individuals who may attune instruments that may be in accord with certain lengths that are of a certain wave vibration, so that these are in unison, then there is the perfect accord for the bringing of those influences or forces into the experiences of individuals who may hear, feel, see, experience those activities that are *without* their *own sphere* of activity, but brought into their relationships as one to another by the use of those forces that must work by a law.

1135-3

The sender in telepathy

The process of telepathy is closely tied to the creation and nature of thought forms. As mentioned in the section on fundamental assumptions, the mind is able to pattern or shape energy, and the product of that process is a fourth-dimensional thought form. Thoughts are things, in the sense that they are very real and continue to exist after they are no longer consciously held in mind. When the sender in a telepathy experiment focuses his or her mind on a

34

target—whether it is a particular symbol, a specific picture, or a physical ailment in his or her own body—it is perceived through the sensory system. Often this involves the use of more than just the sense of sight. In many telepathy experiments the research methods have been designed to enable the senders to make use of as many different senses as possible, by having them smell, taste, touch or listen to the target as well as look at it. The following diagram depicts the primary steps involved in the creation of the sender's thought forms.

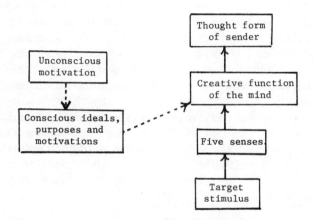

Just as conscious attitudes and ideals have a significant influence on the *receptive* function of the five senses (see the section on awareness of subjective, inner events), they have an important directing effect on the creation of the sender's thought forms. And, once again, we should consider the fact that unconscious motivation often lies behind conscious attitudes and purposes.

The readings suggest that certain attitudes, purposes and motivations are optimal for the creation of thought forms; if these are part of the sender's mental makeup, impressions of whatever target he is focusing on will be more likely to be received. Among these helpful attitudes are the desire to grow in spiritual awareness, a sense of relaxation (as opposed to straining to send the telepathic message), and a belief that the psychic contact can be made. Conversely, certain other conscious or unconscious attitudes and motivations, like fear, anxiety and skepticism, may block the psychic communication.

It is interesting to note, as well, that sending and receiving are apparently two separate processes, and frequently a person will be better at one than the other. This is mentioned in the following passage:

Not all elements may be attuned to a vibratory influence sufficient for sending or receiving. Some may send while others may receive. There may be those that are able to do both. 1135-4

Superconscious awareness

How can we know to what we are psychically attuning? This is one of the most frequently asked questions concerning ESP. The problem of the *sources* of psychic information was often brought to Edgar Cayce, for many individuals who received readings were concerned about the origins of their own personal psychic experiences. Some felt that they were attuning to discarnate souls— that is, individuals who had died physically but continued to be alive in another dimension of reality. The evaluation of such sources is, of course, especially relevant to any consideration of mediumship. In the following passage, we see that the readings suggest that some people who die do not realize for a while what has happened. Having discarded their flesh bodies, they may be experiencing in their finer physical bodies; yet they continue to try to contact or affect the three-dimensional, material world.

Just as an entity that leaves the earth's plane oft experiences an interim without the knowledge of being *without* that dimension; being in a greater dimension, yet not capable of manifesting again in its form in a third dimension, seeks to express itself. This we see in many phases, in many manners. 311-2

The reader might wonder how such contacts with discarnates should be included in our model of how ESP works. Probably the most effective way to answer this would be to consider such discarnate souls as "senders." Even though they may not have flesh bodies, the creative function of the mind is still operative and thought forms are created. These thought forms can potentially be picked up telepathically by a receiver, just as can be done in more traditional telepathy experiments.

However, the readings warn that these discarnate entities do not necessarily offer good advice or accurate information. A person who has died is not necessarily smarter nor more spiritually attuned than before. Furthermore, it is recommended that we seek guidance from the divine within ourselves rather than from some outside source.

Here again we have the distinction between seeking the superconscious awareness and focusing on some of the more limited levels of universal awareness, which may be occupied by discarnate souls. This is one reason why automatic writing, for example, is *not* recommended. In terms of our model, automatic writing would involve an individual allowing the thought forms of another to direct the activities of both the spiritual centers and certain structures of the body. This influence can grow to such an extent that movements of the flesh body are controlled by the outside entity. This differs from inspirational writing, in which a person attunes to the divine within and then writes, using his or her own conscious mind and will.

When individuals worried that they might be picking up on thought forms of discarnate or evil forces, the readings suggested a specific technique for protecting oneself.

Q-2. How can I discern the helpful entities or forces from those forces that would do me harm?
A-2. In each experience ask that they acknowledge the life, the death, the resurrection of the Jesus, the Christ. They that answer only as in the affirmative; otherwise, "Get thee behind me, I will have no part with thee. Through His name only *will* I, [422], *accept* direction!" 422-1

Thus the intuitions are well, provided these are tempered in spirituality—not ism.

For, as these vibrations come about the entity, know that if ye surround yourself with the creative forces or vibrations that are the way, the truth and the light, then *only* good may come; and those things of dire natures, or demoniacal forces in any form will not be a part of thy experience.
2539-2

Once we properly understand the role of discarnate souls and don't make the mistake of assuming that souls on the other side are generally wiser and more spiritual than we are (which may be inherent in many forms of spiritualism), we can explore the nature of superconscious awareness. As has been mentioned, this is the source of information that the readings recommend. Because it is beyond the limitations of time and space, superconscious awareness has access to all knowledge.

For example, contained within the superconscious are the *likelihoods* of future events. For this reason, the most effective way of demonstrating prophecy, or precognition—in which a person makes a guess concerning the nature of some future occurrence—is to attune oneself to the superconscious. Of course, we must be careful not to imply that everything that will happen is fixed, for this would deny free will. The readings are very clear in stating that we have free will and that not even God knows what we will choose; however, through our *past choices* we have created strong likelihoods, or probabilities, that specific future experiences will come about.

In a similar way, information about all other kinds of events and conditions is accessible to superconscious awareness. This includes knowledge of things not yet known by any other person (which could serve as the target in a clairvoyance test) or of whatever is being held in mind by someone else (a possible target for a telepathy test). Referring back to our consideration of the sender in a telepathy test, this means that the thought form created by the sender is known to superconscious awareness. This is illustrated in the following diagram:

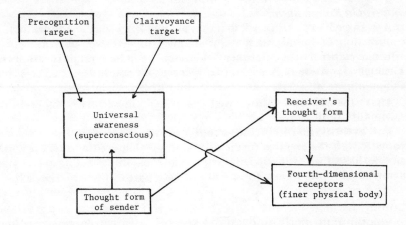

As we can see, this aspect of our model illustrates a principle which has been mentioned previously: There are two primary ways in which a psychic contact can be experienced. One of these is to think of the other person or source of information as being *outside* of oneself; this method involves an attempt to receive impressions through a matching of personal thought forms. The other approach is to affirm that the source of psychic information can be found *within* oneself. This second alternative asserts that once an individual has attuned to superconscious awareness, the psychic information that will be most helpful will be given. In the following passages we see that the second method is recommended. The reader

38

will note that in the first of these passages (and in several other excerpts) the general term "universal consciousness" is used. A thorough study of the many readings given on the nature of mind and of psychic ability seems to indicate that such references to universal awareness are intended to denote the superconscious mind.

What is the *source* of the information as may be had in such experiments, that goes beyond that called or termed the ordinary mind guessing? Or what is the basis of telepathic or clairvoyant communication? . . .

To be sure, the experience is a portion of the Mind; but Mind, as we have given, is both material *and* spiritual . . .

It is not then to be presumed, supposed, or proposed, to be a calling upon, a depending upon, a seeking for, that which is without—or that outside of self; but rather the attuning of self to the divine within, which is (the divine) a universal or *the* universal consciousness.　　　792-2

Q-1. On March 2nd, whose voice did I hear speak to me, and what was the message?

A-1. . . . To be sure, this was a manifestation—but rather than being specific, rather than being an entity activity from without, it is rather the awakening within of the abilities to so associate and so connect and communicate with those influences from without. Then, as given of old, if there will be held and magnified within the consciousness of self that that desired, that voice, that presence that would aid in bringing the various consciousnesses to self, must be from the universal influences, or from His messenger, then this may be magnified in self and for self. Be mindful that it is not clothed in some other power.　　　262-40

The reader may be wondering if every psychic impression that comes from superconscious awareness is therefore pure and uncontaminated. This is not the case. For example, the readings given by Edgar Cayce claim to have come from superconscious awareness, but there seem to be instances in which the personal memories or thoughts of Edgar Cayce filtered in. In other instances, an impression coming from the superconscious of a psychic may draw upon the receiver's memories and thought-form images as a way of assuming a symbolic form that can be transmitted to conscious awareness. However, in such a case, the thought forms of the receiver are playing a very different role than they do in the kind of telepathy in which the sender's and receiver's thought forms must match. In this matching type of telepathy, there are distinct limitations as to what can be transmitted, because the range of information that can get through is limited by the kinds of experiences and memories available to the receiver.

Perhaps an analogy would clarify this difference between the two types of telepathy. Imagine that you have a very important complaint that you wish to make to the President of the United States. Let us suppose that you call the White House and you are told that your complaint will be relayed to the President through his Chief of Staff. You might not care for this course of action, because you know that the transmission of your message will be only as accurate as the intermediary person is willing and able to make it; you will be dependent on his having had experiences similar to your own and on his being capable of recreating your frustrations and suggestions and expressing them articulately to the President. At worst, the Chief of Staff might even disagree with your opinions and either distort the message significantly or block it from getting through at all.

A superior alternative in this situation would be for you to have a personal audience with the President. Let us imagine that this audience can be arranged only under the condition that the Chief of Staff is permitted to be in the office with you and the President. An additional stipulation is that after you have presented your complaint and suggestions, the Chief of Staff might choose to express his opinions on the matter as well. In this case, however, your message will have gotten through to the President directly, even though his mind may also be somewhat affected by comments made by this third party. As the reader has probably surmised, the citizen with the complaint represents the thought form of the sender; the Chief of Staff, the thought forms of the receiver; and the President, the receiver's finer physical body.

The readings go on to suggest ways in which we can judge whether or not we are attuning to superconscious awareness. If we feel drained after a psychic experience or at the end of an ESP test, we are probably not attuning ourselves to this highest source.

This may be set as a criterion to any—yes, to all: When such an experiment, such a trial, draws or tires, or makes the mind foggy or dull or become as a drain upon the physical energies, know you are attuning wrong—and static has entered, from *some* source!

For the universal consciousness *is* constructive, not destructive in *any* manner—but ever constructive in its activity with the elements that make up an entity's experience in the physical consciousness.   792-2

According to the readings, the capacity to make contact with the divine within oneself is the highest form of psychic ability. In a society that is still highly impressed by phenomena and the *results* of attunement, such as psychic readings and psychokinesis, this concept might not be fully appreciated nor understood. However, the fulfillment of our potential to know directly the divine is what the readings place at the pinnacle of psychic experience.

Q-1. What is the highest possible psychic realization . . . ?
A-1. That God, the Father, speaks directly to the sons of men—even as He has promised. 440-4

A second way in which we can judge whether or not we have attuned to superconscious awareness concerns the quality of the impression we receive; more specifically, it involves evaluating the nature of the guidance contained within the information. Superconscious awareness will always direct us to take the very best possible action available to us. The importance of this principle cannot be underestimated in our personal efforts to develop psychic ability. The evaluation of possible psychic impressions is a problem which we will all face, and even as gifted a psychic as Edgar Cayce wrestled with this very question, especially in the early years of his work. Often an intuition or a hunch may direct us to do something which we can justify as permissible or acceptable; and yet, we are encouraged in the readings to use a higher standard of judgment. Simply stated, the question which we should pose to ourselves is this: Is this information or guidance directing me to do the very highest or most loving thing possible? Whenever the answer to this question is no, we are probably best off to seek further within ourselves and attempt to contact a source of psychic information that can meet this standard.

Finally, in our consideration of the role of superconscious awareness, we should keep in mind the confusion in meaning among these three words: mystic, psychic, and occult. What does each of these terms signify about attunement to the superconscious? The readings make the following simple distinction. The mystic experience is a contact with the Spirit or superconscious mind *without* a simultaneous expression in the physical world. For example, in a trance-like state of ecstasy a person may come in touch with the Infinite, but at that moment he loses contact with his finite physical self. The occult, on the other hand, is limited to psychic *phenomena*—experiencing the *effects* of higher-dimensional reality, without necessarily having an experience of their origin. Attending a séance and having what sounds like a dead relative's voice come through a medium would be an example of an occult experience. The psychic, when experienced in the way recommended in the readings, involves both an attunement to the superconscious *and* a simultaneous expression in the physical world and conscious mind.

Q-1. . . . What is meant in the life reading by "Do not confuse the mystic, the psychic, the occult forces," and how is this to be accomplished?
A-1. Each of these terms—mystic, psychic, occult—represent phases of experience in the human experience acting through the mental body, the spiritual body, the physical body. While each of these are one, as the Father, the Son, the Holy Spirit—the Body, the Mind, the Soul—mystic is as the spirit or the *activity,* while the psychic is the soul, the occult is the mind. Do not confuse; for each in their respective sphere—if and when taken alone—becomes confusing.
The occult is phenomena, or phenomenon. Alone considered it may become confusing.
If the mystic or the mysterious is considered alone it may become confusing. 1265-3

This reading suggests that there is a temptation inherent in each of these three experiences. In each case this involves taking too limited a viewpoint. For the mystic, the problem arises if he fails to integrate his profound experience into daily life and human relationships. For the occultist, the problem comes if he fails to hold a spiritual ideal in seeking such experiences and becomes preoccupied with the phenomena. The temptation faced by the psychic is twofold: (a) to *lose* his sense of balance between the mystical and the occult by focusing too much in one direction, or (b) to forget that his psychic attunement must be with something inside himself rather than with an outside source.

Actions in the material world
The final aspect of our model of how ESP works concerns the *application* of a psychic impression. This involves taking an inner experience and translating it into physical expression; the expression can be a verbal response, like guessing a telepathy target or making a prediction about some future event, or a specific action, such as buying a particular stock because of a dream that one hopes was psychic in nature. In order to make our model comprehensive, we will also want to indicate actions that are based on either perceptions from the material world or impressions from

42

imagination and memory. The following rather complex diagram accounts for these various possibilities:

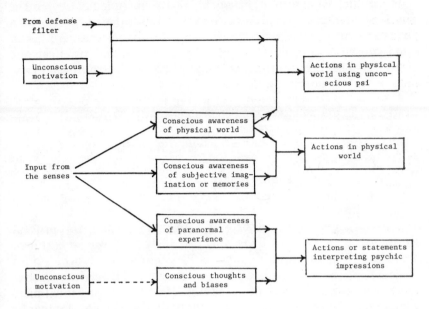

Although this aspect of our model may appear rather imposing to some readers, it is relatively easy to follow if we begin with the point labeled "Input from the senses." If the senses are receiving information primarily from the outside world, then the first of our three types of conscious awareness is created; this awareness is indicated by the box labeled "Conscious awareness of physical world." If the senses are selecting information that comes directly from the individual's own thought forms, this creates the second alternative, indicated by the box labeled "Conscious awareness of subjective imagination or memories." A third possibility is shown in the diagram by the box labeled "Conscious awareness of paranormal experience," which may be the result of the senses selecting information that has come from superconscious awareness or from thought forms created by another person.

This, of course, is a simplified picture, in that the mind is capable of handling a mixture of these three types of conscious awareness simultaneously. For example, it can be cognizant of events in the material world and at the same time bring a specific memory into consciousness. For our purposes, however, the situation can be shown more clearly by separating these three kinds of conscious

43

awareness, though we must keep in mind the limitations that almost always arise when we construct a model.

Three kinds of action in the world are also included in the model. The first of these is represented by the box labeled "Actions in physical world." These actions include behaviors that are based upon conscious awareness of the material world and/or conscious awareness of inner, subjective thoughts. This is the traditional view of how we operate in the world.

A second possible category of action results from coupling the conscious awareness of the physical world with *unconscious* psychic impressions. Here we introduce the effect of psychic impressions that have been stopped by the defense filter (see the section on filtering factors). How much influence this filtered information has probably depends to a large degree upon unconscious motivation to make use of these impressions. This impulse may be strong enough to give this psychic input an extremely significant role in determining our actions in the world. In simpler terms, this process amounts to using our ESP unconsciously. As was mentioned previously, research studies done by Rex Stanford and others have shown that the unconscious use of psychic ability does in fact happen in a wide variety of situations. It is not yet possible to say conclusively how frequently an individual's actions might be affected by unconscious ESP. However, the readings would suggest that in *most* conditions and behaviors psychic ability is used to some degree, although we are rarely aware of it.

A third type of action in the physcial world results from the conscious awareness of paranormal or psychic information. Such conscious psychic impressions must be translated into behavior if they are to have meaning. It is important to realize that this translation also involves conscious thoughts and biases that already exist. The following example should clarify this process and show how it can be a source of difficulty. Let us imagine that a psychic who is asked to predict what will happen during the next year closes her eyes and sees the image of an elephant falling down and dying. Suppose that this is in fact an accurate psychic impression, a symbolic portrayal of a likely future event as perceived from superconscious awareness. In this case, as with many psychic impressions, the information from the superconscious is mixed with thought forms from the unconscious mind of the psychic, creating a symbolic representation that comes into consciousness. To continue our story, suppose that the psychic then makes the verbal statement (i.e., an action interpreting the impression) that the Republican Party is going to be badly beaten in the next election. If, in fact, it turns out that during the next year a terrible disease wipes out half of the elephant population in India, this will indicate the probability that the psychic has misinterpreted her accurate impression. Though she may claim to be totally impartial, her unconscious biases and motivations would perhaps be the most likely cause of this misinterpretation.

In many ways it is what happens *after* the psychic impression comes into conscious awareness that separates the effective psychic from the ineffective one. This process of translating intuition into words and deeds is the test of how useful psychic development will be. In some instances, our psychic information may stimulate us into forceful activity; in others, the act of keeping silent and waiting may be indicated as the most effective use of the impressions. The readings tell us that in either case, keeping our minds focused on conscious thoughts of love and service is the best way of insuring that our actions will accurately reflect the impressions we receive.

Limitations in the Theory

The reader may have noticed shortcomings in specific areas of the theory that has been proposed. One such problem is our incomplete understanding of the exact way in which the finer physical body and associated thought forms are able to interact with the flesh body. In essence, this is one form of the classical mind-body problems: What is the nature of the connection between mental things and physical things? However, this difficulty is not limited to the theory of ESP derived from the readings; no generally accepted answer has been proposed anywhere, and psychology, as well as parapsychology, usually skips over this issue. The readings are noteworthy in that they suggest possible locations for a part of this interaction—within the spiritual centers and the endocrine system, as well as within the connection between the sensory-motor and autonomic nervous systems. Some readers may be particularly interested in this question of how things that are nonmaterial are able to interact with the material world. One especially promising theory, proposed by Evans Harris Walker (1975), makes use of the principles of quantum mechanics.

Another shortcoming of our theory may be in explaining how psychokinesis (PK) works. This phenomenon involves using only the mind to affect things in the material world directly (in common parlance, "mind over matter"). Though the readings are not as clear on how PK operates as they are in explaining the other forms of psychic ability, it almost undoubtedly involves the thought forms of an individual. It may well be that the thought forms associated with a particular spiritual center are most likely to be related to PK. The theory that poltergeist phenomena—the activity of "ghosts" that have an effect on the material world—may be a form of unconscious PK would seem to indicate that the center involved is either the gonads or the cells of Leydig: such poltergeist phenomena are frequently associated with an adolescent child who is going through dramatic endocrine changes, especially in these two glandular centers.

In summary, a comprehensive model and theory of psychic ability has been proposed in this chapter. It has several features usually not included in theories of ESP: the finer physical body, the spiritual centers, and the influence of ideals. An abbreviated version of the overall model appears on the following page. Having studied the individual aspects of the model, the reader can now put all the pieces together and see how they work as a whole.

In Part II we will explore specific procedures and elements of a life style that will facilitate psychic development. These techniques and methods of application should be much more meaningful to the reader who *understands* more clearly *how ESP works*.

A Model of How ESP Works

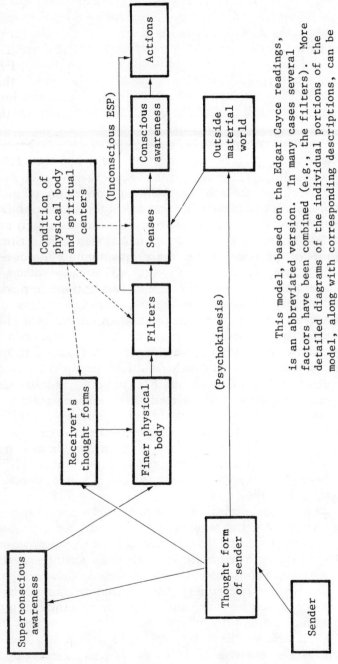

This model, based on the Edgar Cayce readings, is an abbreviated version. In many cases several factors have been combined (e.g., the filters). More detailed diagrams of the individual portions of the model, along with corresponding descriptions, can be found in the sections of Chapter 2.

The solid arrows in this diagram indicate information transfer, while the dotted arrows represent directing influences.

Part II
DEVELOPING OUR ESP

Having explored the theoretical approach to psychic ability put forth in the readings, we can now turn our attention to more practical aspects of the development and use of these faculties. Our model of the mechanism of psychic ability is rather complex; and yet, having first studied ESP from a theoretical viewpoint makes a consideration of practical steps more meaningful. For each procedure and exercise in this section, we already will have developed a rationale or a way of explaining how and why it works. Too often parapsychologists and mind-control instructors are primarily concerned with a technique rather than with the principles and mechanism that allow the technique to work.

In this section we will explore two categories of practical aids to psychic development. The first consists of attunement procedures to facilitate ESP. These include activities that can be incorporated into a person's daily life style, such as meditation and maintaining a proper diet. If you are serious about developing your psychic ability, it will be helpful for you to adopt as many of these procedures as possible. There is reason to believe that even with only a month of application these techniques can facilitate the enhancement of ESP. A daily check-off list is a good way to keep track of your application of these various activities.

The second group of suggestions to be presented is a set of specific training exercises from the readings that can help an individual discover his psychic potential. In considering these exercises we will be exploring particular avenues through which an accurate psychic impression may reach conscious awareness. Some of these exercises have been described explicitly in the Cayce material; others have been created using as a basis principles explained in the readings. Each of these foundation principles has been stated in the previous section. An example of the latter type of technique is a simple sensory-deprivation exercise that is based upon the readings' description of the role the sensory system plays in ESP. Whereas the attunement procedures are to be incorporated together into your life style and applied as frequently as possible, the training exercises are designed to be done one at a time. You may work with them in whatever order you wish.

The following quote should perhaps be our starting point in a consideration of developing psychic ability. It simply says that we can expect results, because we all have this latent capability and it can be developed.

When one develops muscle and brawn for the ring, or for any activity of such nature, there are certain rules of living that must be adhered to, or that have been found to be necessary for such an one to adhere to.

When a faculty of the body, as a pianist, or cornetist, or an artist, is to be developed, there are certain courses of development, certain training through which the body-physical, the body-mental, shall pass as *training* self for such an undertaking.

When one, then, is to develop a faculty, or a force, that is present—as any of these referred to, lying latent in one form or another in *every* individual; so, then, do the psychic forces, the psychic faculties, lie dormant or active in every individual, and await only that awakening or arousing, or the developing under those environs that make for the accentuation of same in the individual.

As the psychic forces are manifesting, or do manifest through the senses, or those portions of the physical being that are trained for acuteness, as is one that would be trained for art in the applying or the mixing rather of color, as one that gets the color, or the tone from the violin, or the like, these are percepts of faculties of the sensory organism, and are akin to the soul.   5752-1

Chapter Three
ATTUNEMENT PROCEDURES FOR THE ENHANCEMENT OF PSYCHIC ABILITY

1. Self-analysis and ideals. This is the starting point for almost every topic covered in the Edgar Cayce readings. We are encouraged to consider our past experiences and current conditions—to engage in self-analysis—and then to specify a direction in which we want to unfold and grow in consciousness—to set an ideal.

A small group of individuals who were interested in conducting telepathy experiments received readings from Edgar Cayce. In one such reading we find the following admonition, which is pertinent to our present work in developing ESP.

Q-1. Please suggest the type of experiments which may be conducted most successfully by this group.

A-1. Well, you would have to take each as an individual—to say as to which may be the most successful! For there are grades, there are variations. There are in the group, as has been indicated, curiosity, wisdom, folly, *and* those things that make for real spiritual development. They each then require first—self-analysis! *What* prompts the individual to seek, engage, or desire to join in such experiments? 792-2

Consider this question in relation to your own life and write your answer in the space below: What prompts you to seek to explore the nature and development of ESP?

In the following three passages, setting and holding to a spiritual ideal is recommended as an initial step in awakening psychic ability.

Q-2. As each name is called, please give suggestions for that particular individual in carrying on his or her part of this group work: First, [1406]:

50

A-2. This entity's experience and experiments will only be altered or hindered by self, and it may go as far into the field as is desired—so long as it keeps God and Christ *as* the ideal.   792-2

Q-3. What can I do to bring about greater psychic development during my present sojourn?
A-3. Self-analysis, and application of the tenets of the ideals that ye find latent and manifested within self.   2934-1

Q-3. What is the exact means or method by which I can consciously reach the divine power of psychic force that is within me and draw upon it for the knowledge, strength, power and direction to accomplish great deeds that will bring about desired ends?
A-3. This lies latent, of course, within self. First find deep within self that purpose, that ideal to which ye would attain. Make that ideal one with thy purpose in Him.   2533-1

Take time to consider what your own spiritual ideal might be. What is the highest spirit that you would like to have guiding every aspect of your life? You may have had a few experiences in which you feel you have caught a glimpse of the highest truth within yourself. What is this perspective of life, this feeling or this spirit of living? Choose a word or a short phrase that describes it or reminds you of it (e.g., God, oneness with life, Creative Forces, freedom). Don't be concerned with what someone else might think your word or phrase means. Be sure to remember that the *words* are not your spiritual ideal—they only represent it.

Write a word or phrase descriptive of your personal spiritual ideal:

This is the spirit that you will want to have guiding your exploration of psychic ability, as well as every other part of your life. Further work with ideals would involve specifying attitudes of the mind and activities of the body that would help you *express* your spiritual ideal in your daily life.

Many statements in the readings link the development of intuitive and psychic abilities with ideals. In one case there is the indication that a reverie type of experience ("those inner flows of consciousness that are aroused by the association of ideas with ideals") would be helpful.

The entity will find that its *own* intuitive forces should be the more often the controlling influence in its activity; that arise through the entity's own meditation, the entity's own concentration upon plans or ideals; whether in relation to its own activities or those of others; those conclusions to which the entity arrives by its own inner urge . . .

. . . Hence it becomes as a pilot, as a criterion for many as they seek along those inner flows of consciousness that are aroused by the association of ideas with ideals that partake of spiritual enlightenment. 1023-2

This passage seems to refer to a procedure that is different from meditation. Since meditation involves a *quieting* of the conscious mind and ideas, it can be distinguished from a thoughtful reverie, in which an individual allows specific ideas and plans that have to do with the *application* of his spiritual ideal to come to mind.

Try this as an attunement procedure once you have set a spiritual ideal: Find a quiet place where for approximately five minutes you will not be disturbed. Focus for a few moments on just your spiritual ideal. Then allow to come into your mind thoughts, ideas and images about how you could more fully express your spiritual ideal in the life situations you currently face. Record in the space below any thoughts or ideas that come to you the first time you use this procedure.

2. Attitudinal changes. Of course, one of the attitudes most likely to be significantly helpful in advancing psychic development is an *enthusiasm* for the self-study and work involved. You have taken the first step in that direction by showing interest in this project and reading this far!

However, this important factor of enthusiasm must be coupled with at least two other key attitudes: trust and willingness to serve. Many people can tell of incidents in which they had an intuitive hunch and unfortunately failed to follow it. This kind of lack of trust in one's own developing psychic abilities can be a difficult stumbling block for anybody to overcome. Just as we must fall a few times to learn the balance necessary to ride a bicycle, we must be willing to trust our emerging psychic ability, even if it means making a few mistakes at first. Gradually we will learn the avenues from within that are most reliable and the quality, or "feel," of an impression that is likely to be an accurate psychic one. The readings recommend listening to these intuitive flashes so that we can learn to develop them into a more permanent psychic faculty.

Q-2. How may I project a counterpart of my conscious awareness to any given place desired and comprehend or even take part in events there?
A-2. . . . These come, then, as flashes to a conscious mind. They may be gradually sustained, maintained. Just as mind may be projected. 2533-8

Jot down any instances you can recall from your own experience in which you had an intuitive flash that should have been trusted because it turned out to be correct.

An attitude of wanting to help others is also important. A sense of giving is the central feature of the following formula from the readings on psychic development.

How develop the psychic forces? So live in body, in mind, that self may be a channel through which the Creative Forces *may* run. How is the current of life or of modern science used in the commercial world? By preparing a channel through which same may run into, or through, that necessary for the use in the material things. So with the body mentally, physically, spiritually, so make the body, the mind, the spiritual influences, a channel—and the *natural* consequence will be the manifestations.

How best, then, to develop those latent forces in one *now,* those who have reached the years of maturity or responsibility in self? Let that mind be in you as was in Him who thought it not robbery to make Himself equal with God, yet took on Himself the burden of all, that through His physical suffering, His privation in body, in mind, there might come the blessings to others. Not self, but others. He, or she, that may lose self, then, for others, may *develop* those faculties that will give the greater expression of psychic forces in their experience.   5752-2

3. Physical exercise. Exercise has the potential to enhance psychic ability in two ways. First, it provides a beneficial influence for the general physiological condition, and it can especially help make the sensory system more attuned and alert. Second, it can have a balancing effect on the activity of the endocrine glands and therefore on the higher-dimensional receptors of the finer physical body (via the spiritual centers).

The following routine was recommended for one individual, though you should use whatever form of exercise you find most beneficial:

Of mornings the body should rise early. First take the full setting-up exercises of the body, upper and lower, circling the body from hips up, bending from hips, stooping from hips, circling arms, head and neck. Then be rubbed down well over the spine with very cold cloth (wet) and then rubbed until the body glows from the blood and circulation being brought to these portions. Do this each morning. 137-1

Check *Edgar Cayce's Handbook for Health Through Drugless Therapy* by Harold J. Reilly for other recommended exercises.

Write down the type and amount of physical exercise that you could, for attunement purposes, reasonably include in your *daily* life:

4. Dietary recommendations. What we feed our bodies is closely related to our state of consciousness. There are general dietary recommendations from the readings which promise to make our bodies more attuned, and thus more apt channels for the expression of psychic development. Many of the recommendations have to do with the avoidance of certain combinations of foods. A more detailed description of these principles will be found in *The Normal Diet* (available from the A.R.E. Press), but briefly stated they are as follows. Jot down next to each one the degree to which you would be willing to incorporate that principle into your daily diet.

a. Eliminate all meats except fish, fowl and lamb.

b. Eat very few foods that combine starches with sweets, such as cakes and pastries.

c. Eliminate overly refined or processed foods.

d. Avoid fruits and vegetables that are picked before ripening on the vine.

e. Avoid the combination of milk and citrus fruits.

f. Avoid the combination of whole-grain cereals and citrus fruits.

g. Avoid the combination of coffee with milk or cream.

h. Eliminate the combination of starches and proteins.

i. Eat 80% alkaline-producing foods (e.g., most fruits and

vegetables) and 20% acid-producing foods (e.g., meats, cereals and starches).

5. Castor-oil packs. Greater physical attunement can also be experienced by the periodic use of external castor-oil packs, especially in the lower abdominal area. This procedure was recommended for a wide variety of physical ailments, and many people use castor-oil packs as a preventive measure to keep their bodies in good shape. The warm oil of the pack stimulates the lymphatic system to do more effectively its work of eliminating wastes and toxins.

The first passage below is a typical recommendation of castor-oil packs. In the second, there is a report of a pack directly stimulating a psychic experience.

First we would begin with the use of hot castor-oil packs for about an hour each day for at least three days a week. These would be applied especially across the abdomen in the caecum or in the right area of the body.

Following each three-day period of using the packs, we would take pure olive oil internally; not too great a quantity in the beginning, but as much as the body may assimilate. 2451-1

Q-7. Please explain the following experience: When taking a castor-oil pack, as I dozed, I began to feel paralyzed, unable to move, speak or hardly breathe. At first I fought against it—as I relaxed I began to feel as though I was moving into space, and that I had great power concentrated in my eyes. Talked with my father, knowing I had the power to influence him to do what I felt was best, yet knowing I should not. A dog sat beside him and then came toward me as if hypnotized, powerless to stop even when we both commanded him to stop. Then I was home and saw the scraps of bacon in the skillet multiplying and growing—recognized the growth as manna known to the children of Israel, which I could pick up in my left hand, but vanished when I touched it with my forefinger and thumb of my right hand. Felt elated that I could describe manna to the Tuesday night group.

A-7. This was an inter-between emotion, or—as indicated—a partial psychic experience.

Consider that which takes place from the use of the oil pack and its influence upon the body, and something of the emotion experienced may be partially understood.

Oil is that which constitutes, in a form, the nature of activity between the functionings of the organs of the system; as related to activity. Much in the same manner as upon an inanimate object it acts as a limbering agent, or allowing movement, motion, as may be had by the attempt to move a hinge,

a wrench, a center, or that movement of an inanimate machinery motion. This is the same effect had upon that which is now animated by spirit. This movement, then, was the reflection of the abilities of the spirit of activity as controlled through the emotions of mind, or the activity of mind between spirit *and* matter.
This was a vision, see? 1523-15

6. Spinal adjustments. Another aspect of the physiology of psychic experience involves the communication between the cerebrospinal nervous system and the sympathetic nervous system. The former especially relates to the activities of the *conscious* mind; the latter, to those of the *subconscious* mind. As we have seen in the previous section, psychic ability involves the conscious mind becoming aware of information accessible to the subconscious mind. The physical expression of this is in the connections between the cerebrospinal and sympathetic nervous systems. This principle is found in the following passage:

Q-1. What is the peculiar sensation felt in left temple?
A-1. Psychic forces as applied to the expression of self, related to those nerves as find expression through that portion of the body. The tingling as is caused is the response of the cerebrospinal with the sympathetic . . .
69-2

There is a primary point of contact between these two nervous systems in the area of each spinal vertebra. When the spinal column is out of alignment it can cause a disturbing pressure on nerves in this area. This kind of difficulty can create a wide variety of physical symptoms, and the readings suggest that such a condition is often at the root of psychological problems as well. Individuals who complained of disturbing and *imbalanced* mental or psychic experiences were often told in the readings to get a series of spinal adjustments to correct the problem.

Q-3. How often should the osteopathic treatments be given?
A-3. This will depend upon the needs of the body. As we find, the *better* manner is to have treatments for two or three weeks, then a rest period for a week or two weeks, and then begin with the treatments again—these at least twice a week. This adds to the body, allowing the adjustments. For manipulative forces osteopathically given, unless there is necessity for corrections, only assist the body in breaking up congestion or congested areas or in assisting ganglia under stress or strain to be so adjusted that the eliminations or drainages in portions of the body are set up and stimulation

to active functioning organs is produced. These have been given properly. If the body will adhere to those suggestions in a *consistent* manner, we will find relief in same.   1110-4

7. Gems and stones. For some people certain types of stones may provide an attuning influence which will enhance psychic ability. In the following reading we find the principle that a stone can work in two ways: by *emanating* a helpful vibration and by *drawing* vibrations from the outside.

We would then find that the one [stone] that is the nearer in accord to the vibrations of the body that may use same would be the more effective with that particular body.
Yet the very *nature* of the thing [stone] makes it effective with any— *any*—human body, you see; but the more effective with one that is more in accord, or whose positive and negative vibrations are according with the stone itself, see? for it [the stone] throws off as well as draws in ... through the positive-negative vibration. This assists, then, in the unison as a relationship ... hence, as given of old, use such for the abilities to become more of all those influences called in the present psychic, clairaudient, or any of those vibrations that build up or "step up" a body. [Such vibrations are] Also effective, of course, in bringing to the body the abilities to become more effective in giving out of itself, for activity in any of these various directions.   440-18

Various types of lapis were the stones most frequently recommended for psychic attunement. Usually individuals were told to wear the stone against the skin in the throat or heart region; in some cases, however, there was a warning to encase the stone in crystal. If you try some form of lapis, such as malachite, azurite, lazurite or chrysocolla, and find that it is irritating or disturbing, do not hesitate to remove it.

8. Bible study. The readings approach the Bible as a guidebook to spiritual growth and as a historical account of man's attempt to attune once again to the Infinite. If we consider psychic ability as the capacity to draw upon the awareness of the soul, then the Bible can be especially helpful, providing principles and examples for psychic attunement. The fourteenth through the seventeenth chapters of John, for instance, were frequently recommended, for in these chapters Jesus states the fundamental principles and promises about discovering our relationship to the divine. Another frequently recommended passage was the thirtieth chapter of Deuteronomy.

The following excerpt from the readings suggests that answers to our questions and concerns are best found within ourselves, not in any outside source.

Q-6. *Are there any exercises you can give me for the development of my faculty of intuition?*
A-6. Much might be given, but ye are ready for little of same yet. Find first thy relationship to thy Maker. This ye may find, probably, best in interpreting in thine own experience the 30th of Deuteronomy, the 14th, 15th, 16th and 17th of John; knowing, as ye read same, it is *you*, thyself, [815], being spoken to—by the spirit of truth that is expressed there. Not in the mere words that are said, but in the spirit that moved those entities in giving expression to man's individual soul-relationship to God.   815-7

Q-4. *How can I get well-educated, kind and refined associations?*
A-4. Read the Book, if you would get educated. If you would be refined, live it! If you would be beautiful, practice it in thy daily life!   3647-1

Reading the following Biblical passages, which give examples of the use of psychic ability, might well help you in your effort to develop those faculties: John 14-17; Deuteronomy 30; John 4:5-19 (telepathy); John 9:1-11 (healing); Daniel 2:19-49 (precognition); Genesis 41:1-32 (precognition); II Kings 6:1-7 (psychokinesis); and Exodus 3:1-4:17 (psychokinesis *and* clairvoyance).

9. Spending time in nature. Psychic ability is a natural function, according to the readings. Perhaps no environment is better suited to facilitate psychic development than the out-of-doors in its natural state. Spending time alone in nature, especially periods of contemplation and meditation, can be an effective aid in attunement.

10. Recording dreams. Psychic ability involves contact with aspects of the mind that are usually unconscious, and the safest and most direct way to explore the unconscious is through our dreams. Many people first discover their psychic potential in a precognitive or telepathic dream. The discipline of writing down dreams is extremely valuable, for we frequently do not recognize the psychic quality of a dream until weeks after we have had it. If we haven't recorded the dream we will likely have forgotten large portions of it. In addition, for most people writing down dreams is associated with increased dream recall.

11. Meditation. Probably the most powerful tool for faciliating psychic development is meditation. Not only can psychic impressions arise during meditation periods, but, more importantly,

we can attune ourselves in meditation so that psychic and intuitive abilities will be more available in our daily affairs and in our dreams. This concept is found in the following excerpts from the readings. The first is a statement that psychic visions may arise in meditation. In the second we find the principle that ESP comes naturally as a result of purification, especially through meditation. The final passage warns that psychic development through meditation should not be for materialistic purposes; in other words, meditating on which stock to invest in in order to get rich would be a misguided use of this aid to attunement.

These become hard at times for the individual to visualize; that the mental and soul may manifest without a physical vehicle. Yet in the deeper meditations, in those experiences when those influences may arise when the spirit of the Creative Forces, the universality of soul, of mind—not as material, not as judgments, not *in* time and space but *of* time and space— may become lost in the Whole, instead of the entity being lost in the maze of confusing influences—then the soul visions arise in the meditations.

987-4

Q-4. I would like to develop psychically. Would it be wise for me to push this development? If so, in what way?
A-4. Rather would we push same through those applications of self to first *understanding* and study of the laws pertaining to the *mental* and *spiritual* phenomena; as manifested in the mental and spiritual experiences of individuals. For these expressions then as psychic forces may be found manifesting themselves through one or the other of the seen forces or influences that make to the material individual an expression of awareness in the individual experience. Whether it takes on the form of an innate consciousness or feeling or vibration or communicative forces that are inspirational in their association and activities in the experience of individuals.

But first, as in those things which we have given in meditation, study to know what to thy mind is dedicating of self's abilities in every way and manner in which they may express themselves to the spiritual forces.

Study to know the manner in which the body, the mind, may be purified or may be consecrated, that there may be the greater expression. And we will find that these developments will come *naturally* of themselves. In their expression, as we find, they will come rather as visions in the ministering to, the listening to, the needs and the activities of others. And in the counsel and the aid the entity may give to such as seek through these channels for aid to self-expression.

319-2

Q-3. What must she do that she may develop her psychic abilities?

A-3. Psychic is of the soul; the abilities to reason *by* **the faculties or by the mind of the soul.** And when this is done, enter into the inner self, opening self through the ideals of the meditation that have been presented through these channels, and surrounding self with the consciousness of the Christ that He may guide in that as will be shown thee; either in writing (inspirationally, not hand-guided) or in the intuitive forces that come from the deeper meditation, may there come much that would guide self first. Do not seek first the material things, but rather spiritual guidance, developing self to the attunement to the psychic forces of the spheres as through the experiences in the varied activities in the varied planes of experience, but over in the light of that promise that has been given to be known among men, "If ye love me, keep my commandments, that I may come and abide with thee and bring to thy remembrance those things that thou hast need of that have been *between* me and thee since the foundations of the world!"

513-1

Briefly stated, the readings approach meditation as the focusing of our attention upon our spiritual ideal. The use of an affirmation, one or more sentences in length—for example, "Let me ever be a channel of blessings to others"—is recommended as a way of capsulizing our personal spiritual ideal. Whereas prayer is the outpouring of thoughts from the conscious mind, in meditation we seek to quiet the conscious mind, making it still and receptive. In order to do this, we should first of all find a comfortable and quiet place for the physical body, and then turn the mind inwards, no longer attending to stimuli from the outside world. After a short period of preparation, including, perhaps, breathing exercises for relaxation, chanting or prayer, we turn our attention to the affirmation. We repeat the words of the affirmation once or twice, attempting to experience the meaning or feeling of the words. Meditation, as it is described in the readings, is *not* repeating words over and over again to force an altered state of consciousness. Instead, it is holding in *silence* the spirit that is awakened by the affirmation.

A person just beginning to meditate should strive to learn *consistency,* even if that means meditating for only five minutes daily at first. It is better to meditate daily for five minutes than irregularly for ten. Most people work up to the point of meditating for at least fifteen to twenty minutes a day. A further study of meditation may be found in *Meditation and the Mind of Man* (available from the A.R.E. Press). As a beginning step in making a definite commitment to meditate regularly, answer the following questions.

What time of day could you devote regularly to a period of meditation?

What might be a good affirmation for you to use in meditation at this time?

12. Search for God Study Group. If we see psychic development in the context of spiritual growth, the work with the lessons in the Search for God material can be an important part of enhancing ESP. It is interesting to note that this material was given for a group of people who came to Edgar Cayce asking for information on developing their own psychic gifts. Out of this request came these 130 readings, which form a step-by-step development sequence focusing on the broader perspective of soul growth.

The purpose of a weekly Study Group meeting with fellow seekers is not specifically to share psychic experiences. Rather, the tremendous value of this particular type of group endeavor lies with the nature of the material itself. The reader will recall from Chapter Two that the ideals and attitudes of an individual play an integral role in awakening psychic ability. The Search for God program is designed to help people reorient themselves to those ideals and attitudes that are most likely to lead to balanced, helpful psychic experiences.

Study Groups meet regularly in hundreds of cities and towns throughout the United States and in many foreign countries. Further information, including the location of groups near you, may be obtained by writing the Study Group Department, A.R.E., Box 595, Virginia Beach, Virginia 23451.

Chapter Four
EXERCISES FOR DEVELOPING PSYCHIC ABILITY

In previous sections of this booklet we have examined the theory of psychic ability and suggested specific attunement aids that may facilitate ESP. In this final section we will explore six training exercises that may prove useful in enhancing psychic development. Some of the activities will undoubtedly fit your individual nature better than others, but for the fullest exploration of your psychic potential you should try each of them at least once. Since some of the exercises are to be applied for a number of days (like the first one, which is recommended for a 20-day period), you may wish to work on more than one of them during those times; there is no reason why you shouldn't do so. Some of the procedures can be completed in just a few minutes, but you may find that you get results only after several days of trying.

We suggest that you approach these exercises with a sense of *openness* and *exploration.* Please try to let go of expectations that might block the development of your potential. In addition, try to keep a sense of excitement and playfulness, rather than becoming overly serious about the various ESP tests. Research has shown that for most people, ESP comes through more effectively when the test has a game-like format, instead of a dry, laboratory one. This is *not* to say that the ESP tasks lack meaning. Simply try to keep in mind that even the most important task can be done with a feeling of excitement and playful exploration.

It is probable that not all of the exercises will work for all people, simply because we are unique individuals and no single technique fits everyone. These six exercises are not the only ways to experience psychic development. They are, however, specific approaches based on the readings that might work for you, *especially* if they are coupled with the *attunement aids* presented in the previous section.

For each exercise you will find (a) a description of the principles involved, (b) instructions concerning how to do the activity, and (c) a suggested way of testing the exercise to see if it works for you. (You may find it helpful to make a record of your experiences with each of these six exercises.)

1. Partnership exercise.

This is a specific technique for developing telepathy. It involves choosing one person who is willing to work with you for 20 days. The two of you will need to agree upon a time of day when you can work on this exercise for five to ten minutes; ideally it would be at the same time each day, but if your schedules do not permit this, it is all right to vary the time. An important factor is to do the exercise *each day* during the 20-day period. The procedure is described in the following reading:

Q-6. Give . . . the principle and technique of conscious telepathy.
A-6. The consciousness of His abiding presence. For, He is all power, all thought, the answer to every question. For, as these attune more and more to the awareness of His presence, the desire to know of those influences that may be revealed causes the awareness to become materially practical.

First, begin between selves. Set a definite time, and each at that moment put down what the other is doing. Do this for twenty days. And ye will find ye have the key to telepathy. 2533-7

One important question about this technique concerns the meaning of the words "what the other is doing." For the purposes of this training exercise we suggest that this phrase be given a broad interpretation, one that can include: (a) what the person has physically been doing just before the time for telepathically tuning in (e.g., I sense that my partner was recently talking on the phone to a relative), (b) how the person is feeling physically (e.g., I sense that my partner has a mild headache), (c) how the person is feeling emotionally (e.g., I have the impression that my partner is angry at someone), (d) what the person has been thinking about (e.g., I have the impression that my partner is thinking about financial pressures he currently faces), and/or (e) what the person has been planning for the rest of the day or for the future (e.g., I sense that my partner is planning on going out to dinner tonight).

You will want to choose as your partner a person whom you are not likely to be near for at least a few hours before the agreed-upon time of day. If you have spent a couple of hours listening and talking to your partner just before you try to tune in psychically, most of your impressions will be not ESP, but simply memories of what you've just seen or heard. It's fine to choose a family member as a partner, but if you do this, select a time of day when you are usually apart. For example, if one of you has a job away from the house, you might try to select a five-minute period while you are apart because of this. If you choose a partner who is not a family member, it should be easy to meet the requirement of having been separated for several hours before doing this exercise. In the event that you and your chosen partner are rarely away from each other physically, let your time of day be immediately upon arising in the morning, before any verbal communications have occurred. In this case you might especially try to tune in to the dream experiences your partner has just had.

In working on this exercise for the five or ten minutes daily, it is *not* necessary to differentiate the moments when you are the sender and your partner is the receiver from those when your partner is the sender. You can both receive from each other *simultaneously*. As you do this exercise, jot down the images you have picked up. Some time after the tuning-in period each day, share your impressions with each other in person or by phone. The sharing does not have to be done immediately following the exercise. This feedback process may be very helpful in learning to distinguish accurate psychic impressions from images that arise simply out of your own imagination. It would probably be worth while for you to record significant instances in which you seem to have telepathically communicated, along with any specific principles you discover about your own telepathic abilities (for example, "I am more likely to accurately pick up physical ailments of my partner," or "I tend to be more telepathic on days when I've just had a good night's sleep").

2. Sleep suggestion.

Prehaps the most direct and safest avenue to universal awareness is through dreams. Of course, not all dreams contain verifiable ESP; nor do all dreams come from universal awareness. In the following two passages are some recommendations on how we might facilitate dream experiences that are psychic in nature.

Whether the body desires or not, in sleep the consciousness physically is laid aside. As to what will be that it will seek, depends upon what has been builded as that it would associate itself with, physically, mentally, spiritually, and the closer the association in the mental mind in the physical forces, in the physical attributes, are with spiritual elements, then—as has been seen by even those attempting to produce a certain character of vision or dream—these follow much in that; for another law that is universal becomes active! Like begets like! 5754-3

Q-18. What is the difference in suggestion to the subconscious mind and the conscious mind?
A-18. Suggestion to the conscious mind only brings to the mental plane those forces that are of the same character and the conscious is the suggestion in action. In that of suggestion to the subconscious mind, it gives its reflection or reaction from the universal forces or mind or superconscious forces. 3744-2

The first passage states the general principle that in the dream state we are attracted to experiences that correspond to what we have built with the mind. In the second passage the technique of suggestion is specifically referred to, and we are told that suggestions directed to the subconscious mind, such as those we might make to our own subconscious as we fall asleep, can evoke a response from the universal mind, or the superconscious.

There is in the readings a large amount of information on suggestive therapeutics—that is, one individual giving suggestion to another in order to help that person with physical, mental or emotional problems. The majority of these cases recommend presleep suggestion (especially for children), indicating that the period of time in which a person is falling asleep is especially conducive to suggestive influences.

This principle can be used to facilitate psychic development. As you begin to feel yourself drifting off towards sleep, repeat several times in your mind a suggestion that you have written beforehand.

The suggestion should affirm that you will be guided by universal awareness; also, it should refer to the specific area in which you would like to receive psychic guidance. For example, suppose you want to know what is really at the root of Mrs. Smith's irritating behavior and what you could do to help her. Your suggestion upon falling asleep might be: "I will be guided by God's wisdom to understand Mrs. Smith and how I can aid her." The response you receive may come through a dream, or it could be a hunch or impression you have upon awakening. It may come as telepathy (e.g., becoming aware of something troubling Mrs. Smith that she has been afraid to verbalize), clairvoyance (e.g., perception of a physical problem that Mrs. Smith isn't aware of), or precognition (e.g., an impression of a likely future event in which you will have a special opportunity to help her). It might take several nights of working with this approach before you get results. In addition, the degree of one's sincerity and enthusiasm is likely to have an important effect on how well this technique works.

Try at least two ways of working with this exercise. First, use an inanimate object as a target. Ask a friend to cut out a picture from a magazine and place it in an envelope. There should not be another picture on the back of the one used, as this may confound the experiment. Make sure you don't have any clues about the contents of the envelope—such as knowing what magazine the picture came from. Put the envelope under your pillow or elsewhere in your bedroom. As you fall asleep at night, repeat a suggestion to yourself which will stimulate your psychic perception. This should be written beforehand and be in your own words. An example would be: "I will be able to tap universal awareness and discover the contents of the envelope." Based upon dreams that you recall or intuitive impressions that you have upon awakening, make a guess as to what is shown in the target picture; then open the envelope and check what the picture actually shows. You may want to try this for several nights, using different target pictures.

This exercise can also be used in relation to another person or a real-life situation. This should not be done just for curiosity's sake. The target should be a person or situation for which you have genuine concern and a willingness to work sincerely with whatever psychic information you may receive. Many people feel that there is a self-protective mechanism within themselves that blocks a psychic impression if they are not really ready to use the information that is potentially available. Most likely, the technique of sleep suggestion *alone* will not produce accurate psychic information; it must be coupled with sincerity and a willingness to help.

To apply sleep suggestion to a real-life situation, you would write a suggestion, such as "I call upon the Creative Forces to show me how I can best understand Bill," and repeat it to yourself as you are falling asleep. It's a good idea to keep a record of the dreams or impressions that come as a result of this exercise. If you feel that you have received an accurate psychic impression, try to apply it in some specific way. For example, if you have a dream about Bill that seems to indicate that he is troubled by feelings of guilt, make a special effort to let him know you appreciate and accept him. In most cases, it would probably *not* be best to ask him, "Are you feeling guilty about something, because I had a dream about you to that effect?" What we are looking for is psychic information that will help us change *our* attitudes and ways of acting so as to bring greater healing. Be sensitive to the precise nature of the situation you choose to work with, because sometimes it will be helpful to share the exact dream or impression with the other person, and sometimes, it won't be; therefore, sharing the dream is not a required part of the exercise.

We recommend that you write a summary of your experiences with both ways of applying sleep suggestion.

3. Hypnogogic state.

There is a second exercise by which we can make use of the transitional stage between waking and sleeping to tap our psychic potential. In the previous activity we used suggestion in the transitional period to increase the likelihood that *during sleep* we would have access to psychic material. Now we will explore the possibility of actually *receiving* psychic impressions during those transitions. In the following passages the readings refer to psychic experiences that can come during such periods.

Q-6. What causes the sinking sensation as I drop asleep, causing me to waken suddenly?

A-6. A development of the intuitive influences in the experience of the body. Do not be disturbed at these. Rather open the door, or allow self to drift away in same. Without fear! for you'll learn a lot for yourself through these! 306-2

Q-2. What caused the dark cloud like a roll of black smoke that seemed to envelope me as a child while in bed at night?

A-2. The sensitiveness of the child in that period of its transition. This should have been cultivated. Do not begin such in the present, except from the angle of prayer and meditation. 4006-1

It would be well to heed the warning given in the second passage above. We should be working with prayer and meditation daily if we choose to explore psychic experiences in the transitional period. Such a discipline makes it more likely that the experiences which come will be helpful and constructive.

There are, of course, two transitional periods. The movement from waking to sleeping is called the hypnogogic state; the one from sleeping to waking is called the hypnopompic state (although in recent times it has become common to refer to *both* periods as "hypnogogic"). In this exercise we will focus upon the latter. Our effort will be to pay careful attention to impressions or feelings that come just as we are beginning to awaken. This can be done by lying in bed a few extra minutes in the morning, allowing the mind to wander and perhaps produce dream-like images. Occasionally you may even seem to drift back to sleep or to a state in which apparently irrational thoughts and ideas arise. By taking time to attend to this special state of consciousness, you may be able to receive accurate psychic impressions.

You can test this state using the same methods you did for sleep suggestion. An unknown picture in an envelope makes a good target to work with at first. If you wish to try this experiment with an actual person as the target, follow the same guidelines as before regarding your sincerity of purpose. You can choose the same individual as before, or select a different person.

You may want to try the following procedure, which some people have found to be a helpful tool in exploring the hypnogogic state. As you are awakening in the morning, lie on your back and place one of your elbows on the bed next to your waist. Bending your arm at the elbow, extend your forearm upward and hold it in a vertical position. Keep it in this position and allow yourself to drift back into the hypnogogic state. If you start to fall asleep, your arm will fall from the vertical position onto your stomach and awaken you. At that point it is to be hoped that you will be able to recall what was going through your mind just before you were re-awakened.

Once again, you may find it helpful to write a summary of your experiences with this exercise using the hypnogogic state.

4. Repetition of a physical task.

Recall that in constructing our model of the mechanism of psychic ability we saw that the readings give the sensory system a central role in the recognition of psychic guidance. In order to perceive psychic information, one of the things that we must do is to allow subjective, inner impressions to come into conscious awareness. We have seen that stimuli from the physical environment often override these inner impressions. This process is illustrated below.

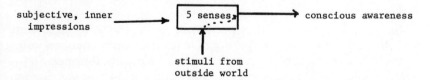

In a later exercise we will work with a procedure to try to cut off environmental stimuli. However, another effective approach may be to make the environmental stimuli as repetitive as possible. Perceptual psychology has found that the conscious mind turns its attention to that which is unusual. For example, if you enter someone's home where there is a grandfather clock, you will probably notice the ticking sound because this is such a novel stimulus. After a few minutes, however, it is unlikely that you will consciously notice the ticking any longer, because the conscious mind tends to tune out that which is repetitive.

It is difficult to determine a repetitive procedure that will work for everyone. However, there seem to be at least two important features that should be included. First, the task should be one that involves some degree of physical repetition; the dances of the Sufi whirling dervishes might be an example of this, since these repetitive movements are used to facilitate paranormal experiences. The task should also involve repetition for the intellectual mind, leaving the more creative, intuitive functions of the mind free to receive psychic impressions. An example of this would be doing a series of arithmetic problems, which, though it is not an especially creative activity, does occupy the rational mind. You may wish to experiment with procedures you think of which include one or both of these features.

One possible exercise using the mind's tendency to tune out monotonous stimuli is an experiment in telepathy that involves you, as receiver, doing a specific repetitive task. Select another person to be the sender for this experiment, and decide what you will use as targets. Among the possibilities are: a deck of playing cards, with which you can try to send and receive the suit or just the color of individual cards; pictures cut out of magazines; and single-digit numbers chosen at random from a phone book (you might use, for example, the last digit of the first entry on randomly selected pages).

As the receiver, your part of the exercise is to perform the following repetitive task while your partner is concentrating on the target. You are to use the spiral pattern which you will find on the following page of this booklet. Place the tip of your index finger on the point marked "start," and then with your finger trace the pathway inward along the spiral. Make sure that your finger stays within the pathway and does not cross over a line. Follow the pathway to the center point, marked with an "X." When you reach the center, do not pick up your finger, but immediately start to trace back outward along the spiral to the original starting point. Upon reaching the starting point, repeat this process and continue to do so. This task will take concentration. When you feel fully into the repetitive procedure of tracing the spiral (it will probably take at least 30 seconds for you to get fully into concentrating on it), momentarily turn your attention to subjective impressions that may come into your mind. Such an impression might be a hunch, a flash, or just a guess that feels as though it has come from something other than your analytical mind. If you don't get anything right away, go back to the tracing and try again. When you have determined your response write it down, and then check with your partner to see if you were right. Attempt several trials with this procedure—between 10 and 25 guesses would be a good number—with a different specific target being used for each new trial. If you are making records of these experiments, you should include (a) the type of targets used, (b) the number of guesses made, and (c) the number of correct responses.

5. Sensory deprivation.

Another approach to facilitating our access to possibly psychic inner impressions involves *cutting off* environmental stimuli. This process is referred to in the following passage:

Each will find a variation according to the application and the abilities of each to become less and less controlled by personality, and the more and more able to shut away the material consciousness—or the mind portion that is of the material, propagated or implied by what is termed the five senses. The more and more each is impelled by that which is intuitive, or the relying upon the soul force within, the greater, the farther, the deeper, the broader, the more constructive may be the result. 792-2

In your own home you probably do not have the facilities to eliminate environmental stimuli completely, but a state of sensory deprivation can be approximated. Cutting out sight and sound is perhaps the most important factor, since our active, conscious minds are largely the product of what we see and hear. The senses of taste and smell are not as developed in humans as in some other animals. The sense of touch, which includes receptors for pressure and temperature, can be largely quieted by lying in a comfortable position in a room with a temperature of around 72 degrees and no wind nor drafts. Considering the living situations of most people, the best time to cut out sights and sounds would probably be between 2:00 and 4:30 A.M. At that time of night it is easiest to find a completely darkened room with a minimal amount of environmental noise.

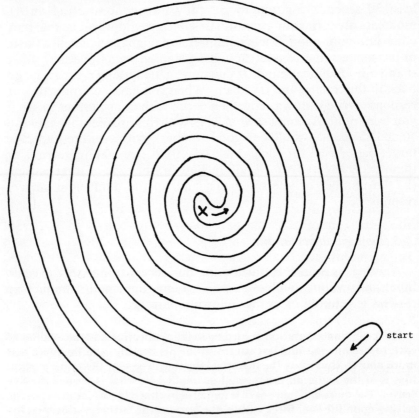

start

Even if you are not used to being up at this hour, it might well be worthwhile for you to try this exercise at least once. Get to bed early, so that you will be reasonably well rested, and use whatever means is best for you to awaken during this period of the night. Find a room or large closet where (a) you can lie down comfortably, (b) you will be exposed to as little light as possible, and (c) as much sound as possible, including the ticking clocks, can be eliminated. You will then be ready to make guesses concerning the nature of target pictures you have previously obtained.

Just as you did in a preceding exercise, ask a friend to cut out some pictures from magazines and place them in individual envelopes. Make sure you are given no clues as to the nature of the pictures. For this exercise five envelopes should be enough. At night, in your state of sensory deprivation, try to guess the contents of each envelope one by one. Hold one envelope in your hands and allow random thoughts or impressions to enter your mind. Continue to do this until you feel that you have received an accurate hunch about the envelope's contents, or until the flow of your impressions creates some kind of recurrent pattern or theme. Then turn on a flashlight and jot down on the envelope your impressions or a specific guess as to the nature of the picture. You may go through all five pictures before opening the envelopes, or you may open each one immediately upon writing down your impressions.

It is suggested that you record a brief description of each target picture and the impressions you wrote down on the envelope. Indicate those that you feel may show some ESP on your part.

6. Decision making.

One of the most significant aspects of psychic ability is that it can help us to make decisions in life. There is, however, no foolproof procedure for obtaining accurate guidance from within. The accuracy of impressions concerning choices in life depends on many

73

factors, such as the degree of one's attunement to universal awareness. Even the soundest technique for receiving psychic guidance will fail if this kind of attunement is missing.

One approach to obtaining direction for life choices is through dreams; we must, however, be careful not to rely solely upon dreams in making decisions. Some dreams can, in fact, be simply wish fulfillment. In the following reading an individual is warned against becoming overly dependent on dreams, especially in times when there is confusion or imbalance in the area of ideals and purposes.

One that has those abilities of vision, especially in dreams. These portend oft to happenings. These are well to consider; yet do not depend too much upon them, unless self is balanced well in its ideal and in its purpose.

3175-1

Dreams do play a role in a more extensive procedure for making decisions. This process, described in many readings, features the use of conscious choice and the turning within for a confirmation or denial of that choice. In the following passage, psychic or intuitive development is linked to this kind of decision making.

Q-11. Give detailed directions for developing the intuitive sense.
A-11. Trust more and more upon that which may be from within. Or, this is a very common—but a very definite—manner to develop: On any

question that arises, ask the mental self—get the answer, yes or no. Rest on that. Do not act immediately (if you would develop the intuitive influences). Then, in meditation or prayer, when looking within self, ask— is this yes or no? The answer is intuitive development. On the same question, to be sure, see? 282-4

Here's a more detailed outline of the steps in a decision-making procedure that, by helping you learn how to get guidance from universal awareness, can stimulate increased psychic development:

1. Set your spiritual ideal. You have already been instructed how to do this in a previous part of this booklet.

2. Pose a question—one that can be answered yes or no— concerning some decision you must make. In working on this exercise, you may choose a simple question or problem that you are currently facing in life, or you may choose one that is of profound significance to you. Whatever problem you decide to work on, write out a question that describes a current decision you are faced with. Be sure to phrase it so that it can be answered by a yes or a no. For example, the question "Should I go back to college?" is much easier to work with than "What should I do now that I have a lot of free time?" would be. The latter is too open-ended and avoids a consciously made choice. Part of our growth in consciousness as souls involves learning how to make decisions properly that are in accord with divine will.

3. Tentatively make a conscious yes-or-no decision in answer to the question you have just posed; in doing this, take into consideration all the information you consciously have access to. Be sure that your tentative decision is one you would be willing to carry out.

4. Measure the tentative decision by your spiritual ideal. Ask yourself, "Could I follow through on my decision and still be true to my spiritual ideal?" If the answer is Yes, you could be true to your ideal, go on to step 5; if it is No, go back to step 3 and try the opposite tentative decision. Occasionally a person finds that neither a decision of Yes nor one of No will allow him to remain true to his spiritual ideal. In that case, the person is not really ready to make a decision on the problem, and he should turn to consistent prayer and a deeper analysis of the decision being faced.

5. Meditate—not on the question, but for *attunement*. With this step we are beginning a process whereby we will seek a confirmation of our conscious decision from within. This confirmation (or denial) is likely to be accurate only to the degree that we have in meditation

attuned ourselves to universal awareness. Do not let yourself be tempted into dwelling on the decision during meditation. Put the question aside and have a period of silent focus upon your affirmation.

6. At the end of your meditation, ask the question and *listen* for a yes-or-no answer from within. This "listening" sometimes elicits a response from an inner voice; at other times, the answer comes as a hunch or an inner impression. Occasionally a person will get nothing at all during this period. In that case, he will want to extend the "listening period" and pay special attention to his dreams. If this is done, a precognitive dream frequently follows, saying, in effect, "If you follow through on the tentative decision you've made, here are the likely results." One can then consciously judge whether or not the likely consequences are acceptable. If they are not, a change in the decision is called for.

7. Measure the decision by your spiritual ideal. After receiving a confirmation or denial, either at the end of meditation or by way of a dream, one should once again check to make sure that the latest understanding of the proper choice does not violate the nature of the spiritual ideal.

8. Act on the decision. No form of psychic or intuitive development has much meaning unless we act upon whatever we receive. Be sure to do this in relation to the specific situation on which you have been working with the previous seven steps.

After going through this exercise you may want to repeat each of the steps, especially if the decision you face is an important one. At the end of the procedure, you might wish to record your question, decision and resulting action, as well as your feelings about this exercise.

Conclusion

The reader who has completed both sections of this book will now have surveyed the basic concepts given in the Edgar Cayce readings on psychic ability.

From Part I there will have been gained insights into the **fundamental principles of how ESP works.** In many ways the principles presented here are quite novel to parapsychology. For instance, the notion that we can understand psi phenomena only by understanding the soul is not generally accepted among parapsychologists. Nor has the concept that there exists a higher-dimensional body to receive psychic impressions have been given general acceptance. The perspective that physical attunement enhances psi is another aspect of the Cayce material that has been adopted by only a few researchers. And although research has indicated that some of a person's attitudes (for example, one of belief in ESP) may affect psychic sensitivity, little research has been done to test the effects of attitudes such as love and the desire to serve others. Here is the point at which the Edgar Cayce readings make their most important theoretical contribution to the understanding of how ESP works. Although research has shown ESP to be associated with an extroverted personality, the readings say that it is more than just a reaching out and an involvement with others that enhances psi. It is the *quality* of that reaching out—a desire to be of loving service—that really makes the difference.

Some readers may not be satisfied with their results in working with Part II of this book. Assuming that you have tried applying these concepts and still have not experienced psychic development as quickly or as fully as you expected, it may be due to one of the following reasons:

1. You may not have given yourself enough time. Psychic development usually occurs over a period of months and years. Some initial gains are frequently observed with just a little work, but the development of accurate, dependable ESP is usually a rather slow, step-by-step process. The serious seeker needs patience. To use once again the analogy of musical ability, consider the time and work required to master an instrument such as the piano or the violin.

2. You may not yet be working with the proper purposes. The readings suggest that ESP comes naturally as a result of the desire to genuinely love and serve others. If you are seeking to develop ESP simply for proof of the phenomena or for selfish reasons, you may be blocking access to those levels of the mind that allow psychic experiences to happen.

3. Perhaps you have not yet properly attuned yourself. The integration of body, mind and spirit is necessary to attain psychic impressions consistently from the superconscious mind. Even if you've begun working with the attunement procedures (such as meditation, dream study and dietary recommendations) referred to in Part II of this book, you may have to devote more energy to them over a longer period of time in order for your efforts to begin resulting in psychic experiences.

We should also keep in mind that when psychic ability begins to emerge, it may not come in the way we expect. A person who hopes to start hearing voices in meditation may instead begin to get accurate psychic impressions in dreams. If such a person isn't open to recognize whatever form of ESP comes about, it may seem to him as if no psychic development has taken place.

As a final note, the reader is encouraged to explore psychic development (in its broadest sense, which is soul development) in the context of a Search for God Study Group. These groups are sponsored by the A.R.E. and are without charge to the participant. The Search for God program makes use of a time-tested approach that provides balance, support from others, and a continual refocusing on the ideal of love and service.

REFERENCES

Ciba Foundation Symposium on Extrasensory Perception. Boston: Little Brown, 1956.

Gammon, M. *The Normal Diet.* Virginia Beach, Virginia: A.R.E. Press, 1957.

Govinda, L.A. *Foundations of Tibetan Mysticism.* New York: Samuel Weiser, 1960.

Honorton, C., and Harper S. "Psi in a Procedure Regulating Perceptual Input." *Journal of the American Society for Psychical Research* 68 (1974): 156-68.

Jung, C.G. *Modern Man in Search of a Soul.* New York: Harcourt, Brace and World, 1933.

Jung, C.G. *The Archetypes and the Collective Unconscious.* The Collected Works of C.G. Jung, vol. 9. Princeton: Princeton University Press, 1959.

Jung, C.G. "Synchronicity: An Acausal Connecting Principle." *The Structure and Dynamics of the Psyche.* The Collected Works of C.G. Jung, vol. 8. Princeton: Princeton University Press, 1960.

Karagulla, S. *Breakthrough to Creativity.* Los Angeles: De Vorss, 1967.

Lilly, J. *The Center of the Cyclone.* New York: Julian Press, 1972.

McGarey, W. *Edgar Cayce and the Palma Christi.* Virginia Beach, Virginia: A.R.E. Press, 1970.

Murphy, G. "Field Theory and Survival." *Journal of the American Society for Psychical Research* 39 (1945): 181-209.

Osis, K., and Bokert, E. "ESP and Changed States of Consciousness." *Journal of the American Society for Psychical Research* 65 (1971): 17-65.

Persinger, M.A. "Geophysical Models for Parapsychological Experiences." *Psychoenergetic Systems* 1 (1975): 63-74.

Puryear, H.B., and Thurston, M.A. *Meditation and the Mind of Man.* Virginia Beach, Virginia: A.R.E. Press, 1975.

Puthoff, H., and Targ, R. "Psychic Research and Modern Physics." In *Psychic Exploration,* edited by E.D. Mitchell and J. White. New York: Putnam, 1974.

Rao, K.R. *Experimental Parapsychology.* Springfield, Illinois: Charles C. Thomas, 1966.

Reilly, H.J., and Brod, R.H. *The Edgar Cayce Handbook for Health Through Drugless Therapy.* New York: Macmillan, 1975.

Rhine, J.B. *Extra-Sensory Perception.* Boston: Humphries, 1935.

Sechrist, E. *Meditation—Gateway to Light.* Virginia Beach, Virginia: A.R.E. Press, 1972.

Stanford, R. "An Experimentally Testable Model for Spontaneous Psi Events, I: Extrasensory Events." *Journal of the American Society for Psychical Research* 68 (1974): 34-57.

Tart, C.T. "The Physical Universe, the Spiritual Universe and the Paranormal." *Transpersonal Psychologies.* New York: Harper and Row, 1975.

Walker, E.H. "Consciousness and Quantum Theory." In *Psychic Exploration,* edited by E.D. Mitchell and J. White. New York: Putnam, 1974.

White, R.A. *Surveys in Parapsychology.* Metuchen, New Jersey: Scarecrow, 1976.